Civil War Mississippi

Civil War
Mississippi

A Guide

Michael B. Ballard

UNIVERSITY PRESS OF MISSISSIPPI / JACKSON

http://www.upress.state.ms.us

08 07 06 05 04 03 03 02 01 00   4 3 2 1

Maps by Becky Smith
All Vicksburg campaign maps are adapted from Michael B. Ballard, *The Campaign for Vicksburg*, Conshohocken, PA: Eastern National Park and Monument Association, 1996.
   The Tupelo map is adapted from Michael B. Ballard, *The Battle of Tupelo*, Murfreesboro, TN: Southern Heritage Press for the Blue and Gray Education Society, 1996.
   The Brice's Cross Roads map is adapted from Parker Hills, *A Study in Warfighting: Nathan Bedford Forrest and the Battle of Brice's Crossroads*, Saline, MI: McNaughton and Gunn for the Blue and Gray Education Society, 1996.
   The Corinth map is adapted from Albert Castel, *General Sterling Price and the Civil War in the West*, Baton Rouge: Louisiana State University Press, 1968

Library of Congress Cataloging-in-Publication Data

Ballard, Michael B.
        Civil War Mississippi : a guide / Michael B. Ballard
            p.   cm.
        "A Muscadine book."
        Includes index.
        ISBN 0-87805-870-2 (alk. paper). – ISBN 1-57806-196-2
(pbk. : alk. paper)
            1. Mississippi–History–Civil War, 1861-1865–Campaigns.
        2. United States–History–Civil War, 1861-1865–Campaigns.
        3. Mississippi–History–Civil War, 1861-1865–Monuments–
        Guidebooks. 4. Mississippi–History–Civil War, 1861-1865–
        Battlefields–Guidebooks. 5. Mississippi Guidebooks.
        6. Historic sites–Mississippi Guidebooks.   I. Title.
        E516.B35   2000
        973.7'3'09762–dc21   99-30825
                                                                    CIP

British Library Cataloging-in-Publication Data available

For my nieces, April, Celeste, and Melody

Contents

Preface

Civil War battles in Mississippi played a major role in determining who won the war in the western theater. This fact has taken on new meaning in recent years as many Civil War historians have argued that the outcome of the entire war was decided in the west. Battles in the eastern theater are more famous and are still more written about than encounters in the west. But the war turned on the consequences of the fighting at Fishing Creek, Kentucky; Fort Henry and Fort Donelson in Tennessee; New Orleans, Louisiana; Island No. 10 on the Mississippi River near the Tennessee-Kentucky border; Murfreesboro and Chattanooga, Tennessee; Chickamauga, Georgia; the Atlanta campaign in Georgia; and several campaigns and battles in Mississippi.

This volume has several purposes. The most important is to inform the novice about the war in Mississippi. I have attempted to achieve this through brief narrative descriptions of the major campaigns and battles in the state. I have also tried to place each campaign and battle within the context of the war in the west and the conflict as a whole. While the book targets the novice, it is hoped that even knowledgeable Civil War buffs and historians will benefit from my attempt to examine the Mississippi war in an expansive framework. At the end of each of the narrative's three parts, suggestions are given for further, more in-depth, reading about the military campaigns. The concluding chapter is an attempt to place the legacy of the war in Mississippi in a perspective that extends beyond the battlefield. The economic devastation and racial upheaval that came with the war sent shock waves through many succeeding generations of Mississippians. The final chapter contains a brief overview of the decades after the war and a comment on present-day thinking in Mississippi regarding this important event. That chapter is followed by several sections providing further information. The first of these offers suggestions pertaining to the touring of campaign sites. (Plans to visit sites should be made well in advance; visitors should always ask about hours of service and possible admission fees when making calls to the various locations.) Remaining sections provide the names of significant battle and other war-related sites, selected lists of minor battles and skirmishes and of Civil War cemeteries and other burial sites, and suggestions for additional places to visit.

PART I
Iuka and Corinth

In the spring of 1862, Union forces in the war's western theater had made significant progress in fracturing a long, and in most places lightly defended, Confederate defense line that extended from western Virginia to the Mississippi River. The line had been breached by a Union victory at Fishing Creek, Kentucky, and had suffered irreparable breaks at Island No. 10 on the Mississippi River and at forts Henry and Donelson in Tennessee. Nashville, the Tennessee state capital, had been evacuated without a fight. So, while Confederate victories in Virginia had led to nothing more than a stalemate in the eastern theater, Union victories in the west had led to a marked occupation of Confederate territory and to massive Rebel manpower and materiel losses that could not be easily replaced.

An emerging northern hero in the west, Ulysses S. Grant, a West Pointer and Mexican War veteran whose prewar endeavors outside the army had failed, now carried his army from Nashville on a southwesterly course toward northeast Mississippi. Union intelligence indicated a large buildup of forces there under the leadership of Albert Sidney Johnston, the Confederate general who had been forced to evacuate Tennessee in the face of Grant's onslaught.

Johnston indeed was gathering an army at the important railroad junction town of Corinth, Mississippi. In early April 1862, he marched his army toward Pittsburg Landing, a site on the Tennessee River about twenty miles north of Corinth, where Grant's army was encamped. Surprisingly, and inexcusably, Grant, though he knew of Johnston's buildup, did not have his army in a good defensive position.

The result was the bloody two-day Battle of Shiloh (the battle got its name from Shiloh church on the battlefield), April 6–7. Johnston's initial attack surprised and shocked Union troops, and the Yankees who bore the brunt of the assault fled in confusion. But after Johnston fell mortally wounded and Union troops made some desperate stands, the Confederate attack bogged down. The next day Grant, buoyed by reinforcements, counterattacked and drove the Rebels from the field.

The Confederates retreated to Corinth and built impressive entrenchments north of the city. Grant, victorious but in trouble with his superiors because of the pounding his army had taken on April 6, yielded command of the army to Henry Halleck. Halleck marched his army slowly toward Corinth, planning to besiege the town. Corinth was strategically significant because of the intersection of vital railroads there—the north/south Mobile and Ohio and the east/west Memphis and Charleston. Stopping every night to dig in, Halleck gave the Confederates plenty of time to prepare for the Union attack. Despite the defensive earthworks his men constructed, P. G. T. Beauregard, the new Confederate commander, decided it would be a forlorn hope for his heavily outnumbered army to try and defend Corinth. With his masses, Halleck could easily encircle the town, cut off Confederate supplies, and ultimately force the surrender of both Corinth and Beauregard's army.

So Beauregard executed a successful ruse to stall Halleck while the Confederates withdrew safely to the south toward Tupelo, Mississippi. Trains periodically rolled into Corinth accompanied by Confederate cheers. Halleck assumed, as Beauregard hoped he would, that Rebel reinforcements were arriving in large numbers. The trains then pulled out carrying troops, the wounded, and artillery safely away from Corinth. By the time Halleck decided to assault the Confederate works, all the Yankees found were empty trenches and a few Confederates left behind to offer token resistance.

Corinth was in Union hands, but Beauregard had saved his army.

Halleck offered only token pursuit and later departed after breaking up his massive army by sending detachments to various other commanders, thus allowing Beauregard to camp unmolested at Tupelo. Grant reassumed command of his army and began solidifying his north Mississippi line. His next target would be Vicksburg.

Vicksburg survived an attack by Union naval forces (see part II, chapter 3) in the spring and summer of 1862, and it became obvious to Union strategists that combined naval and army operations would be necessary to reduce the city. The navy had little competition. With the fall of New Orleans and Baton Rouge, Louisiana, south of Vicksburg, and the surrender of Island No. 10 and Memphis, Tennessee, to the north, Union vessels controlled the river except for fortified points at Vicksburg and Port Hudson. (Another site, Grand Gulf, situated a few miles south of Vicksburg, would be built in the spring of 1863.) On the river itself, the Confederacy had little navy to combat Union gunboats. The only bright spot had been the CSS *Arkansas*, a Rebel ironclad that had created consternation among the Federal navy around Vicksburg. However, the *Arkansas* malfunctioned and had to be scuttled while attempting to cooperate with Confederate forces in a failed attempt to retake Baton Rouge on August 5, 1862.

So the stage was set for the Vicksburg campaign, but Grant waited, planned, and tried to build up his army. Events in Tennessee and, ultimately, Kentucky lay behind his hesitance. Braxton Bragg, who had taken over the Confederate Shiloh army from Beauregard, had invaded Tennessee with the major portion of that army. Bragg's idea was to march through Tennessee into Kentucky in order to sign up anticipated Kentucky recruits. Don Carlos Buell commanded the Federal forces resisting Bragg's advance.

While this campaign unfolded, Grant had to wait and see what Buell might need in the way of reinforcements from Grant's army. Confederate troops still in Mississippi, commanded by Earl Van Dorn at Vicksburg and Sterling Price in northeast Mississippi, also kept an eye on Bragg, considering that they might be on their way to join his army at any moment. Since each side knew the other could be sending additional troops to Tennessee, Grant, Van Dorn, and Price began jockeying to keep their respective opponents from sending men to Buell and Bragg.

Van Dorn left Vicksburg with a small army in September (the Union navy having long since given up its attempt to take Vicksburg) and moved north/northeast. Price marched from Tupelo and on September 13–14, 1862, occupied Iuka, a small town in the northeast corner of Mississippi on the railroad line that connected Memphis and Corinth with Chattanooga, the line by which reinforcements could be sent to Buell (or Bragg). Price had just missed a confrontation with William Rosecrans, who had ordered his army back to Corinth in anticipation of an expected Confederate attack there. Grant found this situation intolerable and prepared a two-pronged movement against Price, thus setting the stage for the Battle of Iuka, and, later, a Rebel counterthrust at Corinth.

Seemingly the war had come to stay in northeast Mississippi, an area that had few slaves and that had been lukewarm toward the secessionist movement. The hard times brought on by the conflict hardened attitudes toward both the Union and the Confederacy.

Silent Guns: The Battle of Iuka

Ulysses S. Grant had become more and more obsessed with Sterling Price's intentions. Was Price trying to block the rail line to keep Grant from sending troops to Don Carlos Buell? Grant knew that Earl Van Dorn was bringing a small army northeastward from Vicksburg, but he had received conflicting reports from his scouts. Some intelligence suggested that Price intended to march into Tennessee and on to Kentucky, no doubt to reinforce Braxton Bragg. Other scouts thought Price had in mind a coordinated attack with Van Dorn against Corinth. Still others suggested that Price would cross the state line into Tennessee in an effort to draw Union troops away from Corinth, and, if that worked, then Van Dorn would assault the depleted Federal force at Corinth.

Given all this uncertainty, Grant characteristically decided to grab the initiative. Van Dorn was still a few days away, so on September 16, 1862, he issued orders for a two-pronged campaign against Price at Iuka. Grant instructed General William Rosecrans with nine thousand men to march south and east via the towns of Rienzi and Jacinto. He was to leave enough troops in Jacinto to protect Corinth's southern flank. Then Rosecrans would swing north and assault Iuka from the south. Meanwhile, General E. O. C. Ord would march his detachment of six thousand down the north side of the railroad between Corinth and Iuka via Burnsville. Ord would attack Price from the north. If the assaults on the Confederates were coordinated as planned, Price would be caught in a Union pincer. Grant travelled with Ord's column; both Ord and Rosecrans began marching to battle on September 18.

Sterling Price. Commanded Confederate forces at the Battle of Iuka. Credit: Ezra J. Warner, *Generals in Gray*, Baton Rouge: LSU Press

Sterling Price waited at Iuka with a force of fifteen thousand split into two divisions led by General Henry Little and General Dabney Maury. Price would be fifty-three years old on September 20. His military training and experience had come in the field, first in the Mexican War and early in the Civil War in Missouri and Arkansas.

Price had been dutifully following his instructions to keep an eye on Grant so that Price could try to block reinforcements sent to Buell. Braxton Bragg had grown so anxious about Grant's potential for bolstering Buell that he had ordered Earl Van Dorn several weeks earlier to join Price. But Van Dorn had lingered at Vicksburg while a detachment of the Vicksburg army, led by General John C. Breckinridge, had marched to attack Baton Rouge. The attack had been unsuccessful, but Breckinridge had taken steps to occupy Port Hudson, a strategically strong Mississippi River town above Baton Rouge. With Breckinridge gone, Van Dorn refused to leave Vicksburg. August had drifted by, and September had come with no concerted action in northeast Mississippi by the Confederates.

On September 1, Bragg wired Price to do all in his power to prevent Rosecrans from marching to join Buell. Price learned that Rosecrans had indeed dispatched a few troops to Tennessee, so Price decided to occupy Iuka, which he did with only light resistance from Union troops. Meanwhile Bragg urged Price to abandon his position and come to Tennessee to counteract Rosecrans's expected arrival there. But Price hesitated, being fully aware that Van Dorn had at last left Vicksburg and was hurrying north. In fact Van Dorn ordered Price to leave Iuka and join forces at Rienzi; from there Van Dorn planned to attack Corinth. Grant's offensive, however, forced Price to fight where he was.

William Rosecrans, known affectionately as "Old Rosy" by his troops, was a West Pointer, class of 1842. He had had no combat experience before the Civil War, having served ten years in the engineering corps before resigning from the army in 1854. The forty-three-year-old general proved to be a solid but unspectacular leader in the field. The imminent battles at Iuka and Corinth would inflate his reputation, which would later be deflated by his resounding defeat at Chickamauga.

Rosecrans executed his part of Grant's plan, most of which had been suggested by Rosecrans, concentrating in the Jacinto area on the evening of the eighteenth. He notified Grant that General David Stanley's division was so exhausted by a forced march that he would delay assaulting Iuka until the next day. This threatened the timing of the joint attacks, so Grant told Ord to attack at the sound of Rosecrans's guns.

At daybreak on the nineteenth, Rosecrans had his two divisions (the other division was commanded by Charles Hamilton) on the march. As the Federals approached Iuka, Hamilton's division took the lead, followed by Stanley's. The column's advance elements drove in Rebel pickets to within a couple of miles of Iuka near a crossroads south of town. Here they found Price's infantry and artillery ready for battle.

Price's day had gotten off to an interesting start. Early on the nineteenth he had received word from Van Dorn to unite their forces at Rienzi. So Price had ordered his army to prepare for a march southwest out of Iuka. At about the same time, Price also received a message from Ord, an "insolent demand," as Price later described it. Ord had received a rather skewed account of the Battle of Antietam in Maryland between Robert E. Lee and George McClellan. At best McClellan had won a tactical victory, hardly the smashing triumph that Ord had deduced from the newspaper version. Ord assured Price that McClellan's great victory meant the end of the war; therefore the Confederates in Iuka might as well surrender. Price replied that even if the news were true, his men would only fight harder for their independence.

In the early afternoon, Price received another surprise message; his pickets on the Jacinto road had been scattered by a large Federal column. This was the first inkling he had of Rosecrans's presence on his southern flank. At around 2:30 p.m., Price ordered General Little to send one brigade, soon followed by another, to meet this threat. Little's two brigades tangled with Hamilton's Federal division, supported by Stanley's troops. Price described the fight as being "waged with a severity which I have never seen surpassed."

Thick underbrush and timber made deployment difficult for the Union brigades, but they fought hard, yielding one battery only after three Confederate charges. Little's men, commanded by General Louis Hébert and Colonel John Martin, pushed the disorganized Federals back some six hundred yards. Price directed Little to call up his other two brigades. At that moment, a Federal bullet struck Little in the forehead, killing him instantly.

Little was a longtime veteran of the U.S. Army, having served with distinction in the Mexican War. Before assuming division command, he had been a member of Price's staff and had served his commander well at the Battle of Pea Ridge in Arkansas. Little had been a special favorite with Price, who emotionally cradled his friend's head

William Rosecrans. Led Union forces at the battles of Iuka and Corinth. Credit: Ezra J. Warner, *Generals in Blue*, Baton Rouge: LSU Press

after the stricken general fell from his horse. Recovering his composure, Price turned his attention back to the battle.

Darkness ended the fighting just as Little's remaining two brigades arrived. The Confederates on the southern front spent the night preparing to renew the attack at dawn. Maury had his fresh troops waiting in reserve, watching for trouble from Ord that never came. Price wanted to continue the fight the next morning, but his subordinates convinced him to leave his position and march to join Van Dorn. Price based his decision on the fact that Ord with a strong force was in his rear. Even if he defeated Rosecrans, Ord's threat could negate the victory. Price ordered his men to prepare to march to Van Dorn at Rienzi.

On the Federal side, William Rosecrans had been listening in vain for the sound of Ord's troops coming to join the fight and catch Price between the Union forces as planned. But Ord, a West Pointer and an experienced soldier, never heard the firing that was to be his signal to charge Iuka from the north. In his campaign report, Ord explained, "The wind, freshly blowing from us in the direction of Iuka during the whole of the 19th, prevented our hearing the guns and co-operating with General Rosecrans." A quirk of nature almost cost Rosecrans dearly.

Early on the morning of September 20, Price began marching his men south on the Fulton road east of the previous day's fight. Rosecrans had done nothing to block the road, a negligence for which he was severely criticized by Grant. It can be said in Rosecrans's defense, however, that he had been engaged in a battle where he had had much difficulty deploying his men. And he had expected help from Ord which never came. Of course, he could have sent out scouts and detachments to fell trees over nearby roads to protect his flanks if for no other reason. Rosecrans did err, but he certainly was not solely responsible for Price's escape.

Price did a superb job of stealing a march on Rosecrans. The Union commander later wrote, "Day dawned. No firing on the front. Our skirmishers, advancing cautiously, found the enemy had retired from his position." Rosecrans marched into Iuka, then sent Stanley in pursuit of Price. The Confederates had such a head start that by evening Stanley considered himself too far behind to continue.

So the vicious battle of Iuka ended with a whimper. Within the few hours of fighting on September 19, Union casualties numbered 141 dead, 613 wounded, and 36 missing. Price lost 86 killed, with 408 wounded. He had to leave behind 485 sick and wounded. (Rosecrans in his battle report insisted that total Confederate casualties, including prisoners and previously hospitalized soldiers, numbered 1,438.)

As usually happened in inconclusive battles, both sides claimed victory. Rosecrans considered Price's exit from the field to be evidence that the Federals had won the day. Price thought that his punishing attack on Rosecrans and his leisurely departure from Iuka, despite being threatened on two sides, gave him claim for victory.

Ulysses S. Grant, angered that Price had slipped away, commented, "Our only defeat was in not capturing the entire army or in destroying it, as I had hoped to do." Grant ordered most of his army back to Corinth, which he expected to be the next Rebel target. Though disappointed, Grant's soldiers had removed the threat at Iuka, for the moment anyway. Grant did not know it at the time, but he had also taken an important first step in securing north Mississippi.

Price's men arrived safely in Baldwyn on September 23, and five days later joined up with Van Dorn in the vicinity of Ripley, southwest of Corinth. From this point, Van Dorn would lead the combined forces on his ill-fated Corinth campaign.

TWO

Van Dorn's Folly:
The Battle of Corinth

In his early forties, the brash Earl Van Dorn cut a fine figure astride his horse. The epitome of the mythical southern cavalier, Van Dorn, a West Point graduate in the same class as William Rosecrans, loved the army life, sought danger, dreamed big, and, all in all, was in many respects the western counterpart to a Virginia cavalryman named J. E. B. Stuart. Appointed major general in September 1861, Van Dorn seemed to have a promising career ahead of him in the Confederate army.

But on the campaign trail, that promise dimmed at the Battle of Pea Ridge on April 7–8, 1862. During this fight in the northwestern corner of Arkansas, Van Dorn demonstrated all the weaknesses that made him an inept commander of a large army. His plans were too ambitious for the resources he had available. He intended to win in Arkansas, and then march as a conquering hero into Missouri, claiming that state for the Confederacy. Such grandiose ideas based on unrealistic means made Van Dorn a reckless battlefield commander.

He demanded considerably more from his troops than they were able to deliver. Not that he had mediocre soldiers; indeed, some of the Confederacy's best fighters, especially Missourians, served under Van Dorn at Pea Ridge. They won the first day's fight, but Van Dorn crippled the second day's effort by ignoring some basic factors. His ordnance train was not where it should have been; his men were worn out and suffering from the bitter cold; his plan of attack,

Earl Van Dorn. Confederate general defeated at Corinth. Credit: Ezra J. Warner, *Generals in Gray*, Baton Rouge: LSU Press

though well designed, had been poorly coordinated, and therefore his army was not in the position he had hoped it would be in; and his Union foes were still very capable and in a strong defensive position. Despite these problems, Van Dorn ordered an assault and was soon leading his defeated army eastward. Van Dorn's performance during the forthcoming Corinth campaign would offer proof of another of his shortcomings—that he learned very little from his mistakes.

Van Dorn had redeemed himself somewhat at Vicksburg. He had arrived in Mississippi with his Arkansas army too late to fight at Shiloh, so he had wound up in Vicksburg, where he took more credit than he deserved for keeping Union gunboats at bay during the summer of 1862. The gunboat threat had ended, the Baton Rouge campaign had concluded with mixed results, and now Van Dorn looked to Corinth for his next great adventure. In fact, he had visions of clearing west Tennessee of the enemy, a difficult if not impossible task given his resources. But that had not stopped him at Pea Ridge, and it would not stop him now.

Sterling Price's army had stopped for a rest at Baldwyn after its retreat from Iuka. On September 28, Price's men finally joined up with Van Dorn and his force from Vicksburg at the town of Ripley, southwest of Corinth. Revealing the nature of his strategic goal, Van Dorn named the combined forces the Army of West Tennessee. The army included Price's divisions under Louis Hébert and Dabney Maury and another division commanded by Major General Mansfield Lovell, who had been scathed in the southern press for giving up New Orleans without much of a fight earlier in the year. Two cavalry brigades led by Frank Armstrong and William H. Jackson rounded out the army of twenty-two thousand. On paper, and in fact, this was a veteran, tough army capable of winning if given proper leadership. As at Pea Ridge, Van Dorn's campaign plan was excellent, but it ignored some factors that would doom his vision of great victory.

In his postcampaign report, Van Dorn acknowledged that scouting information indicated a total Union force of over forty thousand in the west Tennessee-north Mississippi area. But these troops were widely scattered, and Corinth, geographically anyway, was isolated from the rest of the Union detachments. So Van Dorn thought he could hit Corinth, conquer the army under William Rosecrans there, and then, with control of the railroad junction, continue his campaign to rid west Tennessee of Yankee troops. As Van Dorn said, "It was clear to my mind that if a successful attack could be made upon Corinth from the west and northwest, the forces there driven back on the Tennessee [River] and cut off, Bolivar and Jackson [Tennessee towns northeast and north, respectively, of Corinth] would easily fall, and then, upon the arrival of the exchanged prisoners of war [during the early years of the war prisoners were often exchanged on a one-to-one ratio; once a prisoner had been exchanged, he could return to his army], West Tennessee would soon be in our possession and communication with General Bragg effected through Middle Tennessee. The attack on Corinth was a military necessity, requiring prompt and vigorous action. It was being strengthened daily under that astute soldier, General Rosecrans."

It certainly was, and that was one of several holes in Van Dorn's plan. Van Dorn had been in Corinth for some time after his arrival from Arkansas, so he surely knew that the Confederate works constructed there were strong, especially to the north, where Confederate commanders had anticipated an attack by Grant's army after Shiloh. And Van Dorn's own words indicate that he had to know that the Federal army occupying Corinth had been laboring to strengthen existing works, and to build more, since a Rebel attack on the town had been anticipated for some time. Perhaps his scouts had not seen the ring of inner works around the town that U. S. Grant had ordered constructed, but, with so much scouting going on, this does not seem likely.

In addition to the formidable defenses, Van Dorn counted on the size of his army to intimidate much smaller Union detachments scattered around the region. They might be intimidated, and they might fall back, but he did not have enough men to force their surrender, or, more important, to keep them from assaulting his rear once he began his attack on Corinth. Why he assumed the towns of Bolivar and Jackson would easily fall is not clear; probably he figured his mere presence would force the garrisons to evacuate or to raise the white flag. But would these detachments feel obliged to do either, or would they try and help Rosecrans? Further, even if Van Dorn managed to take Corinth, he was counting on a dubious source of reinforcements—exchanged prisoners—to help him hold it and then launch further campaigns. Such prisoners would have to arrive at just the right time, which was highly unlikely, and they would have to be armed and ready to fight at once, which was more unlikely. Finally, Van Dorn was gambling that he could strike Rosecrans and win quickly before Rosecrans could call in all his outposts. If the gamble failed, Rosecrans could assemble twenty-three thousand troops, outnumbering Van Dorn by at least a thousand. That was not a great advantage, but Rosecrans's numbers would be more significant since he would be fighting defensively from behind strong entrenchments. Given the usual pattern of warfare, his force would not have as many casualties as Van Dorn's attacking force, so the longer the fight lasted, the greater the disparity in numbers would be.

Obviously, things had to go just right for the plan to succeed. One essential ingredient was speed, and this particular October in Mississippi had started out unseasonably hot. Van Dorn seemed to ignore the debilitating effect the heat might have on his men, who had a long march to battle. At Pea Ridge, Van Dorn's men had suffered from cold; at Corinth hot, humid weather would be their enemy. Figuring in the human factor in military campaigns seemed beyond Van Dorn's comprehension.

The dye was cast. Early on September 29, Van Dorn ordered his troops to march north from Ripley. He intended to confuse the enemy as to his true intention before turning southeast to attack Corinth. He felt proud of his men as they marched out, confident that he was on the verge of a great victory. The army threatened Bolivar before wheeling right across the Hatchie and Tuscumbia rivers. Van Dorn knew he must move quickly now, that the blow must be "sudden and decisive," delivered before Union troops north and west of Corinth could converge on the Confederate rear.

In Corinth, William Rosecrans was deeply troubled by Van Dorn's presence, mainly because he had been put in the position of guessing the enemy's intentions from a variety of possibilities. Adding to Rosecrans's problem was the lack of a map of much of the territory to the northwest. Rosecrans sincerely hoped that, since the countryside was so rife with rumors of a Confederate attack on Corinth, Van Dorn would send only a masking force, a detachment to occupy Rosecrans's attention and mask Van Dorn's true route. Rosecrans could then brush aside such a detachment, get in behind Van Dorn, and block any attempted Confederate retreat back into Mississippi.

Rosecrans posted troops on the northwestern outskirts of town to provide some flexibility for future movements. On October 3, Rosecrans deployed, from left to right, the divisions of generals Thomas

McKean, Thomas Davies, and Iuka veteran Charles Hamilton along the northwest perimeter, holding his other Iuka division, David Stanley's, in reserve. Rosecrans had already begun calling in detachments from as far away as Iuka. His general plan, he wrote later, "was to hold the enemy at arm's-length by opposing him strongly in our assumed positions, and when his force became fully developed and he had assumed position, if we found it necessary, to take a position which would give us the use of our batteries and the open ground in the immediate vicinity of Corinth, the exact position to be determined by events and the movements of the enemy." In effect, Rosecrans wanted to draw the Confederates toward the Union lines near Corinth in the hope that Van Dorn would throw his men against the considerable fortifications ringing the town.

The first shots of the battle rang out early on the morning of October 3 as Van Dorn wheeled to the right toward Corinth and his advance clashed with Rosecrans's pickets northwest of the town. Van Dorn advanced with Lovell on the right, Maury in the center, and Hébert on the left. Maury and Hébert marched through country bordered on Maury's right by the Memphis and Charleston rail line and on Hébert's left by the Mobile and Ohio. Lovell moved to the right of the Memphis and Charleston.

The skirmishers of both armies put up a tough fight; Rosecrans's skirmish line did not retreat into his outer entrenchments until about 10 a.m. Here the Confederates found before them a four-hundred-yard-long belt of abatis (felled trees with sharpened branches). The Rebel assault began with Lovell charging on the Confederate right, the attack gradually being taken up by Price's troops in the center and on the left. Rosecrans's army finally retreated to their next line of earthworks, but only after holding against Van Dorn's onslaught for three and a half hours. Already Van Dorn's hope for a quick victory was fading.

Now the Confederates faced an even more formidable line of Yankee defenses. Price called them the "most approved and scientifically constructed entrenchments, bristling with artillery of large caliber and supported by heavy lines of infantry." Nevertheless, Price, now making the main assault, sent his veterans forward, and after hard, vicious fighting carried the works, capturing many Union prisoners and two heavy artillery pieces. Rosecrans later explained that he had lost the two guns because his army had not kept its alignment, thus exposing part of his line to flanking fire from the enemy.

Davies's Union division in the center bore the brunt of the Confederate attack. Rosecrans noted he had invited attack at that point because his men there had fallen back farther than the wings of his army. He had to readjust his lines in the heat of battle, moving his forces forward or backward depending upon their proximity to Davies. Finally, as darkness approached, the battered, hard-fighting men in blue pulled back into their innermost, and strongest, trenches.

Sterling Price was justly proud of his men. He had driven the enemy all day, noting that the fighting just before the Federals' final retreat had been "of unparalleled fierceness." The burden of battle had fallen mainly on his infantry, because the nature of the terrain had prevented him from setting up his artillery in effective positions. Price had been close to the kind of victory Van Dorn had dreamed of, but night had come and his men were exhausted and running low on ammunition. As at Pea Ridge, a logistical problem haunted Van Dorn. Delays in getting ammunition from the rear to the front for Price's infantry had helped stall the attack.

On the right, Mansfield Lovell had made impressive gains all day but against much less resistance. His men had cleared outer Union obstacles along the south side of the Memphis and Charleston Railroad and by nightfall had formed on a ridge from which he could launch an assault against southwest Corinth. The timid Lovell stopped short of carrying his attack farther, was ordered by Van Dorn to send forward a detachment to feel out the enemy position, and then pulled his men back in as night fell.

Van Dorn could claim victory this day; his men had pushed the enemy back effectively on all fronts. But he had not won his major objective. Rosecrans still held Corinth, and was building up his force by the hour. Van Dorn admitted the folly of his overly optimistic plan: "I had been in hopes that one day's operations would end the contest and decide who should be the victors on this bloody field, but a 10 miles' march over a parched country, on dusty roads, without water, getting into line of battle in forests with undergrowth, and the more than equal activity and determined courage displayed by the enemy, commanded by one of the ablest generals of the United States Army, who threw all possible obstacles in our way that an active mind could suggest, prolonged the battle until I saw, with regret, the sun sink behind the horizon as the last shot of our sharpshooters followed the retreating foe into their innermost lines." He went on to insist, however, that one more hour's daylight would have secured the victory, a dubious assertion at best.

Van Dorn did not let disappointment keep him from preparing a plan for the next day. It was a simple yet impressive one, but this time two of his commanders, Lovell and Hébert, let him down. The plan called for an incremental attack. First, Confederate batteries set up on a ridge west of Corinth would begin firing at 4 a.m. Next, Hébert on the Confederate left would attack at dawn, swinging his left flank toward Corinth to hit the Federal right. Lovell on the Confederate right was to wait until he heard Hébert heavily engaged, then send two of his brigades on a charge across the lowland southwest of town. Simultaneously, Maury of Price's division in the center would attack head on. To thwart threats from the rear in the direction of Bolivar, Jackson's cavalry would burn the Memphis and Charleston Railroad bridge across the Tuscumbia.

In Corinth, William Rosecrans, convinced by the viciousness of the Rebel attacks that he was outnumbered two to one, continued to pour in reinforcements. His alignment in the inner works consisted of McKean on the left, Stanley in the left-center defending the well-

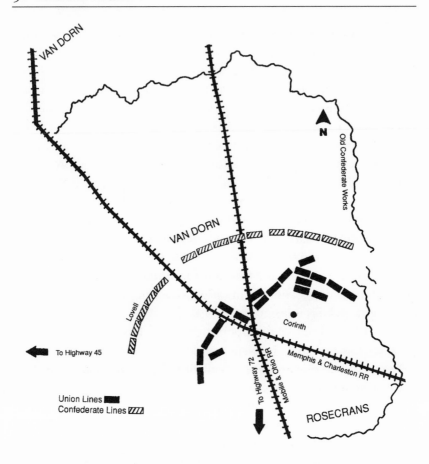

Battle of Corinth, October 3-4, 1862 (Note: Map depicts troop positions early on October 4.)

built batteries Williams and Robinett near the Memphis and Charleston line where it came into town, Davies in the center, and Hamilton on the right. One advantage of having his troops driven into close confines was that when the battle opened they would be close enough together to assist each other on short notice. Tactically, this is known as the advantage of interior lines.

At first all went on schedule for Van Dorn. The cannon opened up, but then daylight came, and he waited in vain for Hébert's attack. One messenger, then two, then three, searched in vain for the tardy general. At about 7 a.m., Hébert arrived at Van Dorn's headquarters with the rather lame excuse that he was too ill to command. Price immediately named Martin Green to take the brigade, but by then Maury's men had engaged the enemy. The battle extended to both ends of the opposing lines from the center. Van Dorn's entire scheme became "disarranged."

As in the first day of battle, Price's Confederates in the center and on the right bore the brunt of the fighting, and were the most effective. The Rebel charges were piecemeal and not coordinated, but the initial charge was quite effective. "One brigade after the other went gallantly into action," Van Dorn recalled. Green's and Maury's brigades drove the Federal troops of Davies, Stanley, and Hamilton into a rout. Rosecrans noted woefully that the enemy came on "in gallant style." He said, "I had the personal mortification of witnessing this untoward and untimely stampede."

Price's yelling troops fought their foes hand to hand in the streets of Corinth, forcing many Yankees to seek safety in houses. The Confederates captured some forty pieces of artillery and overran a Union fortification called Battery Powell just north of town. Price still complained that he was unable to bring his artillery to bear, leaving his infantry to do their best against Federal guns. Their best was extraordinary, but Rosecrans had reserves, and Price did not. So the brilliant attack ground to a halt; Union reinforcements countercharged, and Price's men, fighting without food or water that day, grudgingly retreated, leaving behind most of the captured guns.

Maury's charge against Rosecrans's left center had been particularly memorable, especially the attack on the formidable Robinett. Brave Confederates, notably Colonel William Rogers of the Second Texas, got to the ditch in front of the fort and climbed its walls, enduring a storm of iron and lead produced by equally capable Union

Battery Robinett on Corinth Battlefield. Photo: Michael B. Ballard

soldiers. Rosecrans recorded how the Rebels in front of Robinett charged, reeled back under the hail of fire, then came on again with Rogers in the lead. Rogers fell dead, as did many others, but his bravery was long remembered by those on both sides who witnessed the charge.

What about Mansfield Lovell? Where had he been during all the fighting? The answer appears to be that he, like Hébert, simply decided not to participate. Lovell, born in Washington, D.C., and considered by most southerners to be a Yankee, had been roundly vilified for abandoning New Orleans. A West Point graduate, also in the class of 1842, Lovell had been twice wounded in the Mexican War. Casting his lot with the South, Lovell seems to have lost whatever nerve he might have had in New Orleans. One of his brigadier generals at Corinth, the brilliant John Stevens Bowen, who would make quite a name for himself in the upcoming Vicksburg campaign, noted in his battle report that, Lovell being absent, he took it upon himself to conduct a reconnaissance in force. The upshot of it was that Lovell's division did very little on October 4. Ironically, this may have worked to Van Dorn's favor, because he had a fresh division to cover his retreat.

Van Dorn, despite the two days of brutal fighting most of his army had experienced, entertained notions of retreating south to Rienzi and assaulting Corinth again! Realistic heads prevailed and convinced the commanding general to retreat to Ripley, where the army could take a much-needed rest to recuperate from the grueling campaign. Even the retreat proved to be trying.

E. O. C. Ord's soldiers from Bolivar waited on the bluffs overlooking the Hatchie River bridge, called Davis's Bridge. Maury's men engaged Ord's Yankees in a hard fight while the rest of the army, minus Bowen's brigade, escaped down a country lane called Bone Yard Road. Bowen had remained in the army's rear at the Tuscumbia to challenge Rosecrans's pursuit. Bowen's strong stand at the river drove back the Union forces, and Rosecrans gave up the chase. Van Dorn noted that the rear guard action was carried out "in a manner that reflected great credit on General Bowen and his brigade." Van Dorn might not have been so generous had he known that a short time later Bowen would file charges against his commanding general for the manner in which the Corinth campaign had been carried out. As in most such Civil War cases, a court of inquiry cleared Van Dorn.

The bloody Corinth campaign ended with considerable casualties on both sides. In the three days of fighting, Van Dorn had 505 killed, 2,150 wounded, and 1,812 missing, a total of 4,467, or 20 percent of his army. Rosecrans and Ord together had casualties of 401 killed, 2,334 wounded, and 355 missing, a total of 3,090, fewer than the Confederates but still quite high. Strategically, Rosecrans had won an important victory. With Iuka and now Corinth secure on this front, extreme north Mississippi was firmly in Union hands. Grant could begin planning his invasion of Mississippi to take Vicksburg.

After Corinth, Rosecrans moved on to central Tennessee to take command of the Federal army jousting with Braxton Bragg. Van Dorn was relieved of command and soon was leading cavalry in north Mississippi under a new departmental commander, John C. Pemberton. At the head of horsemen, Van Dorn finally found his niche, and he won long-sought glory by devastating U. S. Grant's supply depot at Holly Springs in late 1862. Unfortunately for the southern cause, Van Dorn's impetuousness, not limited to the battlefield, led to his murder by a jealous husband in 1863.

SUGGESTIONS FOR FURTHER READING

Castel, Albert. *General Sterling Price and the Civil War in the West.* Baton Rouge: Louisiana State University Press, 1968.

Cozzens, Peter. *The Darkest Days of the War: The Battles of Iuka and Corinth.* Chapel Hill: University of North Carolina Press, 1997.

Grant, U. S. *Personal Memoirs of U. S. Grant.* New York: AMS Press, 1972. Reprint.

Hartje, Robert G. *Van Dorn: The Life and Times of a Confederate General.* Nashville: Vanderbilt University Press, 1967.

Johnson, Robert U., and Clarence C. Buel, eds. Vol. 2, *Battles and Leaders of the Civil War.* 4 vols. New York: Century Co., 1884–87.

Kitchens, Ben Earl. *Rosecrans Meets Price: The Battle of Iuka.* Florence, AL: Thornwood Book Publishers, 1987.

Lamers, William M. *The Edge of Glory: A Biography of General William S. Rosecrans, U.S.A.* New York: Harcourt Brace & World, 1961.

PART II

Vicksburg

The Mississippi River was both an economic and a psychological factor for Union and Confederate commanders as they plotted their strategy in the west. For many years, the river had served as a vital waterway for midwestern farmers shipping their goods to the eastern states via the Gulf of Mexico. Development of railroads and canals had lessened dependence on the river before the war. Yet politicians, merchants, and farmers in the upper Mississippi Valley region did not like the idea of the river being closed because of Confederate artillery looming along the banks where the "Father of Waters" flowed through the Confederacy.

For the Confederacy, control of the lower Mississippi was vital to the union of its states. The portion of Louisiana west of the river plus Texas and Arkansas formed the Transmississippi, the part of the Confederate nation separated from the rest by the Mississippi. The Transmississippi states had much in the way of manpower and materiel that the rest of the southern military machine needed. So the Confederacy set about fortifying certain points along the river to prevent a northern invasion. The big problem faced by Rebel strategists was that the South had no navy to speak of, early on or at any time during the war. It proved to be difficult for shore batteries to knock out Union gunboats on the wide river, especially with guns that were not exactly first-rate. The Confederates also made a strategic blunder in scattering their guns along too many miles of river rather than concentrating them in well-selected locations. This typified the southern problem of trying to defend too much territory in the west.

Losses upriver and down soon rectified that situation, however, forcing Confederates into more compact emplacements. Early in 1862 Union gunboats captured Island No. 10 north of Memphis and later Memphis itself. Federal ships raced up the Mississippi from its Gulf of Mexico mouth and took New Orleans and Baton Rouge. By June of 1862, the last line of Confederate defense of the river was getting shorter. It would lengthen later in the year with the establishment of strong fortifications on the southern flank at Port Hudson, a Louisiana town just north of Baton Rouge on the eastern bank of the river, occupied by Confederate forces defeated at Baton Rouge in August 1862. Many miles farther north, Confederates would eventually fortify the Mississippi River town of Grand Gulf. At the time Memphis fell on June 6, 1862, however, Vicksburg was the only stumbling block left for the Union navy to conquer.

Vicksburg, as U.S. President Abraham Lincoln called it, was "the key." Lincoln looked at a map of the river and saw that its hairpin turn in front of Vicksburg would force southbound vessels to slow down and require northbound ships to build up steam to negotiate the currents. This made boats traveling in both directions vulnerable to artillery fire from the Confederate batteries on the shore line and on the high bluffs above the river. Lincoln could see that, beyond the danger to Union shipping, as long as Vicksburg remained in Rebel hands the Confederates would control the surrounding countryside on both sides of the river for many miles, thus assuring that supplies from this area would continue to feed and equip southern armies. No doubt about it; Vicksburg must be taken.

Easier said than done. With its many steep hills and ravines, Vicksburg was a naturally wonderful site for the construction of defensive earthworks. One observer had said of the town, "After the Lord of Creation had made all the big mountains and ranges of hills, he had left on his hands a large lot of scraps; these were all dumped at Vicksburg in a waste heap." If the Confederates built adequate fortifications, Yankee infantry would have a difficult time breaking through.

Contrarily, the terrain north of Vicksburg seemed very inviting to Union navy vessels. The vast Mississippi Delta stretched for miles north to Memphis, and the thousands of acres of lowlands in between were sliced in various directions by myriad waterways. The area frequently flooded, especially during winter and spring rains, which would allow Federal boats to overcome problems of negotiating narrow streams. If gunboats and troop transports could somehow get into the Yazoo River, which ran from the central Delta to where it emptied into the Mississippi just north of Vicksburg, Grant could land troops and attack from that direction. Of course, Confederates, realizing the danger, felled trees to block waterways and hoped for dry weather.

As the western Federal armies and navy piled success upon success in early 1862, it seemed that the Confederacy was powerless to stop them. But if defending such a large expanse of territory posed problems for the Confederacy, attacking over such a broad front presented challenges to the Union. The juggernaut began slowing down after Shiloh and the Rebel evacuation of Corinth, simply because Union commanders decided to redistribute their manpower to attack on more fronts. Ulysses S. Grant was left to rebuild his army, so for a time Vicksburg would have to wait. Any threat to the town would have to come elsewhere, and it did, by the Union navy from the south.

The Vicksburg campaign can best be understood when divided into four phases. First came the spring 1862 attack by Union gunboats. Then came Grant's fall campaign, which involved the invasion of north Mississippi and an attempt to flank the Confederates with William T. Sherman's Mississippi River expedition to a point just north of Vicksburg called Chickasaw Bayou. Grant then launched his spring 1863 campaign of diversions that eventually allowed him to get his army across the river south of Vicksburg. The final phase included Grant's hard-hitting overland campaign into central Mississippi and his siege operations at Vicksburg.

In the spring of 1862, Union Flag Officer David G. Farragut was brimming with confidence. After taking New Orleans in late April without much resistance, he moved on up the Mississippi to Baton Rouge, which surrendered in early May without a struggle. Buoyed by his success, Farragut decided to continue north. Natchez, Mississippi, which was not defended because of its military insignificance, capitulated, and the town's leaders assured the invaders that there was no Confederate property in Natchez and that there had been no official flying of the Confederate flag. Convinced that he would continue to have his own way, Farragut pushed parts of his fleet on north, anxious to get by Vicksburg and into the Yazoo to destroy a Rebel ironclad supposedly under construction (the CSS *Arkansas*).

Brigadier General Martin Luther Smith had recently taken command of the Vicksburg defenses, and he looked anxiously downriver. The detachment in the hill city was not as ready as it ought to have been for Farragut. Smith hoped to have at least six batteries in place before the enemy gunboats arrived. Did he have time?

THREE

Gunboats: The First Attack on Vicksburg

David Farragut had been around and in the United States Navy most of his life, dating back to experiences as a young boy in the War of 1812. Even though a southerner by birth and having two wives from Virginia (not at the same time), Farragut had been in the old navy too long to sympathize with the secession movement. His successes on the lower Mississippi had made him a hero, but Flag Officer Farragut sought bigger game—Vicksburg. He arrived at the Vicksburg scene on May 30, 1862.

Part of his fleet had already been there for some time. S. Phillips Lee, the commander of the naval advance detachment, had demanded the surrender of Vicksburg on May 18. His message had been rejected emphatically both by the city's mayor and by Brigadier General Martin Luther Smith, commanding the Confederate defenses. Hearing of this rejection, Farragut had directed Lee to "keep up a strict offensive blockade . . . firing upon them whenever you discover any work going on in the shape of batteries."

Lee in turn criticized Farragut for not bringing the whole available Union naval force to bear immediately upon the Vicksburg defenses. Farragut responded brusquely, "I have to state that you are entirely mistaken as to my reasons for not bringing up the ships and attacking the town of Vicksburg. I rather temporarily yielded from the force of circumstances than to any opinion I had formed as to the propriety of blockading Vicksburg rather than attacking it, which circumstances were the difficulty of navigating the Mississippi

River with the large vessels and the impression which seemed to pre-
vail with yourself and the officers of the advance division of the in-
adequacy of the force at Vicksburg to take the place."

So thus far the attempt to reduce Vicksburg had amounted to little more than sporadic shelling. Farragut had hoped to at least partially cut off supplies to the city, but that had not worked. He could
try to block supplies arriving from the Louisiana side, but the railroad east of the river connecting Vicksburg with the Mississippi capital city of Jackson was hardly threatened by gunboats. Farragut also
faced the logistical problem of getting sufficient coal upriver to keep
the Vicksburg fleet going. His supply line back to New Orleans was
long and tenuous. Furthermore, he had trouble finding pilots who
knew the intricacies of the treacherous Mississippi. Recently arrived
infantry, about fifteen hundred men commanded by Thomas
Williams, was not deemed sufficient to assault the Vicksburg batteries and bluffs, even when supported by the navy. Finally, Farragut
and his commanders feared that Rebel vessels equipped with ironclad bows that could batter the Union ships were a big risk. So, Farragut explained in a message to the U.S. Secretary of the Navy,
Gideon Welles, "All these considerations induced me to abandon
the idea of attacking Vicksburg beyond harassing it, to prevent the
erection of more batteries." Farragut concluded that he hoped for
both infantry and naval reinforcements to do more. But many days
and weeks would pass before Union forces could severely threaten
Vicksburg.

In Vicksburg, commanders of the Confederate forces were engaged in a game of musical chairs. Mansfield Lovell, the loser at New
Orleans, would eventually be replaced by Earl Van Dorn. For the moment, Lovell ordered Martin Luther Smith, a New York native who
had married a Georgia girl, to take direct command of Vicksburg
and the defenses. Smith, a West Pointer with an engineering background, had been appointed brigadier general on April 11. Almost
exactly one month later, May 12, Smith took over at Vicksburg.

Smith had gone to work at once. For a week he ordered his men to work night and day to build artillery emplacements. When he had arrived, only three of ten battery sites had been completed, and work had begun on a fourth. As for armed infantry, Smith had only one regiment and part of a battalion. By the time Yankee gunboats arrived on the eighteenth, Smith's small force had completed the fourth and had constructed two more batteries for a total of six. Smith had even found time to drill his artillerists. He felt comfortable enough to issue a feisty reply to the enemy's demand for surrender: "[H]aving been ordered here to hold these defenses, my intention is to do so as long as it is in my power."

Smith stated later in his report that he had been inspired by the determination of Vicksburg citizens. "The inhabitants," he wrote, "had been advised to leave the city when the smoke of the ascending gunboats was first seen." Many did depart, but others "determined to remain and take the chances of escaping unharmed, a few of whom absolutely endured to the end." Some insisted that the town should be held, "even though total demolition should be the result."

Smith also hurried to get work on a Confederate ironclad back on track. The *Arkansas* had been under construction at the Yazoo City, Mississippi, shipyard a few miles up the Yazoo River from where it emptied into the Mississippi. Once the *Arkansas* was finished it could threaten Farragut's vessels quickly. But there had been problems. The contractor had suspended construction, mechanics and other workmen were leaving because equipment and supplies were scarce, and iron had been lost, having sunk in the Yazoo. Smith immediately began rectifying the situation, securing more mechanics and supplies and taking steps to recover the lost iron. He was fortunate in that one Captain Isaac Brown, an intrepid sailor, was placed in charge of the *Arkansas*. Smith noted that, after Brown's appointment, "this important work gave me no further concern."

Confederate reinforcements began arriving. Two Louisiana regiments, followed by two more, several companies of cavalry, an artillery battery, and several companies of Mississippians bolstered the defenses. Still, Smith felt uneasy, for most of these men were new troops, "indifferently armed," and, of course, in need of drill. Smith always remembered his nervousness. This was "the most critical period of the defenses of Vicksburg: batteries incomplete; guns not mounted; troops few, and both officers and men entirely new to service, and not a single regular officer to assist in organizing and commanding. Had a prompt and vigorous attack been made by the enemy, while I think the dispositions made would have insured their repulse, still the issue would have been less certain than at any time afterwards."

Farragut continued to battle logistical complications, as well as the problem of guerrillas firing upon the Union fleet from the eastern banks of the Mississippi. Fire from the vicinity of Grand Gulf, Mississippi, provoked General Williams to burn the town, but the local citizenry convinced him that the guerrillas were not residents. Ironically, Grand Gulf would later be fortified by Confederate troops, and batteries emplaced there would be a major source of harassment for the Federal boats.

On May 26, Farragut's guns opened up on Vicksburg for two hours. The Confederates exercised great restraint in responding. Initially, the lack of Rebel response was due to a lack of ammunition. Smith continued the policy, however, to keep his men fresh. Most of the Yankee bombardment did little damage to Confederate earthworks, and, by limiting his return fire, Smith kept his troops ready for any "close and serious attacks."

For the next several weeks, the Union gunboats kept up an intermittent fire. The fire slackened and then ceased altogether for five days, June 14–18, while Farragut waited for mortar boats to churn up the river to Vicksburg. Meanwhile a fleet from upriver, commanded by Flag Officer Charles Davis, came downstream fresh from victory at Memphis and Fort Pillow, a Confederate bastion a few miles north of Memphis. Union strategists had toyed with the idea of landing troops at Memphis and Vicksburg to storm both places in conjunction with the river war, but the idea had been abandoned, mainly because Confederate troops in northeast Mississippi in the Corinth-Tupelo area might launch an assault in the rear of the Union troops. Memphis fell anyway, without infantry participation. Farragut and Davis hoped that combining forces in an all-out gunboat and mortar boat bombardment might produce the same result at Vicksburg.

Farragut did not wait for Davis. Beginning on June 20 and continuing until the twenty-seventh, Union guns on the river kept up an almost incessant fire into the city. This shelling was intended to soften up the Confederate defenses for the major combined bombardment to begin on the twenty-eighth. That day the gunboats steamed in front of the city, and, as Smith observed, "the decisive struggle was at hand." A witness noted, "The roar of cannon was now continuous and deafening; loud explosions shook the city to its foundations; shot and shell went hissing and tearing through trees and walls, scattering fragments far and wide in their terrific flight; men, women, and children rushed into the streets, and, amid the crash of falling houses, commenced their hasty flight to the country for safety." In the end, it was all for naught; the Confederates stood firm against the storm of shot and shell.

On June 26, Davis's advance boats appeared north of Vicksburg, and on July 12 his fleet opened on Vicksburg. They were interrupted on July 15 when the *Arkansas* finally steamed out of the Yazoo into the midst of enemy vessels. For four days the Federals battled the Confederate ironclad, but the *Arkansas* held its own, severely damaging a few Union boats. The fighting continued at a declining rate until July 27, when the Federal navy, seeing that no infantry support was forthcoming, completely gave up the campaign, which had lasted some sixty-seven days.

After the capture of Corinth, Union General Henry Halleck had broken up his massive army, sending detachments here and there across the South. Without that army to threaten Vicksburg, the Federal navy had no hope of reducing the town. Smith, meanwhile, had yielded command to Earl Van Dorn, and Confederate reinforcements under John C. Breckinridge strengthened the hand of the defenders. Buoyed by the Federal retreat, Van Dorn authorized an attack on Baton Rouge by Breckinridge. The assault was unsuccessful, largely because of mechanical failures aboard the *Arkansas*, which had gone downriver to drive enemy gunboats away from the Louisiana capital. The *Arkansas* was abandoned and blown up by the crew to prevent its falling into enemy hands. Breckinridge's attack then stalled in the face of fire from the unmolested Union fleet. A portion of Breckinridge's troops occupied Port Hudson, just north of Baton Rouge, setting the scene for later stages of the Vicksburg campaign. The river corridor from Port Hudson to Grand Gulf to Vicksburg would remain largely under Rebel control for almost a year.

FOUR

Grant's Failures: Vicksburg, October 1862–April 1863

As the fall and winter seasons of 1862 approached, U. S. Grant may often have sat and wondered at his up-and-down career. A solid Mexican War performance, numerous personal problems including several failures in civilian occupations, glory with his capture of forts Henry and Donelson early in 1862, and criticism for being surprised and battered at Shiloh (the second day's victory had done little to restore him to favor in the eyes of his superiors) and for letting Sterling Price escape at Iuka had all contributed to Grant's checkered life. Now, with north Mississippi secured, he looked to Vicksburg, and he had to make some quick decisions. He knew that prominent Illinois politician John A. McClernand, ever a seeker of fame, had persuaded Abraham Lincoln to give him independent command of an army to capture Vicksburg. McClernand would soon be on his way downriver, so Grant determined to beat him to the punch.

He gathered a force at Grand Junction, Tennessee, and drew up plans for an invasion of north Mississippi. At Grand Junction the Mississippi Central Railroad led south through the heart of Mississippi all the way to the capital city of Jackson. Grant decided upon a two-pronged invasion. He would personally lead one wing down the railroad. William T. "Cump" Sherman, Grant's friend and confidant, would lead the second wing southeast out of Memphis to a junction with Grant, probably somewhere near the Tallahatchie River. Grant also ordered troops in Helena, Arkansas, to cross the river and move east.

U. S. Grant. Commander
of U.S. forces in the
Vicksburg Campaign.
Credit: Ezra J. Warner,
Generals in Blue, Baton
Rouge: LSU Press

John C. Pemberton.
Confederate commander
during the Vicksburg
Campaign, October
1862-July 1863. Credit:
United States Military
Academy Archives

It was hoped that the effect of this operation would be to force the Confederates, now led by John C. Pemberton, to retreat deep into the interior of Mississippi. Pemberton's left flank would be threatened, and he simply did not have enough men to take the offensive and attack Grant and Sherman. Pemberton was not by nature an aggressive general anyway. Most of his previous experience as a career army man had been as a staff officer, a job at which he was supremely competent. But his combat experience had been limited, and up to this point in his career he had never commanded a large force in the field. Further, his pre-Vicksburg assignment in South Carolina had demonstrated that southerners did not trust this Pennsylvania-born general. Why Confederate President Jefferson Davis sent a man of such background to command a vital region remains a mystery.

Pemberton watched anxiously as the blue hordes poured into Mississippi. Yankee troops occupied Holly Springs and set up a major supply depot there and then moved on south to Oxford, finally pushing the Confederates all the way down to Grenada where the Rebels dug in on the south side of the Yalobusha River. Grant halted his main force at Oxford to regroup and firm up his supply line. The Helena troops returned to their base once they had helped force Pemberton to abandon the Tallahatchie. Pondering his options as he went south, Grant decided on a radical adjustment to his original plan. He ordered Sherman to take his troops back to Memphis, where they would travel by boat down the Mississippi, land just above Vicksburg, and try to cut the railroad between Vicksburg and Jackson. Sherman's large force in his rear would force Pemberton to abandon the Yalobusha line, and Grant would push on and join with Sherman to attack Vicksburg.

Sherman moved quickly and was soon steaming downriver with a forty-thousand-man army. The new plan looked good on paper, but ominous developments doomed the Federal campaign. The intrepid Confederate cavalryman, Nathan Bedford Forrest, raided Grant's extended supply line up through Tennessee, forcing Grant

Walter Place, Holly Springs. Served as home for General U. S. Grant and his wife during the North Mississippi Campaign of 1862. Photo: Michael B. Ballard

to relocate his main base to Memphis. Meanwhile Pemberton, reacting to a suggestion by one of his officers, ordered Earl Van Dorn on a cavalry raid against the Union supply depot at Holly Springs. On December 20, Van Dorn and his men left the north Mississippi Confederate lines, circled behind Grant's army, and destroyed over a million dollars' worth of supplies at Holly Springs. The Rebel horsemen continued their destructive raid north up the railroad before winding their way back to the safety of Pemberton's lines. A disheartened Grant had no choice but to retreat to Memphis.

Sherman heard of the debacle at Holly Springs, but he decided to proceed with his planned assault anyway. Landing his troops north of Vicksburg along the Yazoo, Sherman pushed his men across swampy Chickasaw Bayou and assailed the Confederate defenses on Walnut Hills. Pemberton had rushed men to Vicksburg when he

William T. Sherman.
Commander of Union
forces at Chickasaw
Bayou and later during
the Meridian Campaign.
Credit: Ezra J. Warner,
Generals in Blue, Baton
Rouge: LSU Press

heard of Sherman's presence. The Confederates had relaxed their
vigilance a bit when the Union navy had earlier withdrawn from the
Yazoo after a Confederate mine had sunk the gunboat USS *Cairo*.
Now came a race to reinforce Martin Luther Smith at Vicksburg.
The ensuing Battle of Chickasaw Bayou raged December 27–29. Finally Sherman had to give up the fight. His casualties had been high,
and he had never really seriously threatened the Confederate defenses. The year 1862 ended with Vicksburg still firmly in Rebel
hands.

The main characteristic that set U. S. Grant apart from most
officers of his day was his tenacity. He had been thwarted so far, but
he determined to remain active and on the offensive. He put soldiers to work trying to dig a canal across De Soto Point across the
river from Vicksburg. Success would give Union vessels a safe bypass
of the Confederate Vicksburg batteries. The project had been initi-
ated by General Williams's men earlier during Farragut's campaign,

but low water and rampant disease had doomed the Yankee ditch. Grant's efforts also failed, this time because of high water flooding the trench.

Undeterred, Grant set in motion the Lake Providence expedition. Crescent-shaped Lake Providence lay on the Louisiana side of the Mississippi, some seventy-five river miles north of Vicksburg. Grant's engineers had the rather far-fetched notion that they could connect myriad waterways from the lake down to the Red River, which empties into the Mississippi south of Vicksburg. Not only could the Union navy bypass Vicksburg, but Grant could float men down to reinforce Nathaniel Banks, who was operating against Confederate troops at Port Hudson. The engineers failed, but their flooding of the countryside protected the right flank of Grant's army later when they marched down the Louisiana side of the river to cross below Vicksburg.

The Union navy also suffered setbacks during the early weeks of 1863. The Union gunboat *Indianola* was rammed by the *Queen of the West* (the *Queen* had been captured earlier by the Confederates), partially sunk, and surrendered to the Rebels. Another Federal vessel, the *De Soto*, was burned to prevent capture.

Grant ignored the losses and continued to weigh other options. He decided on the Yazoo Pass expedition. His engineers broke through a levee in the Yazoo Pass bayou, and Union ships followed the flood waters into the Coldwater River. The Coldwater emptied into the Tallahatchie, which flowed south to join with the Yalobusha in forming the Yazoo near Greenwood, Mississippi. The Yazoo led to a landing north of Vicksburg. The Confederates waited for the invaders at Fort Pemberton, a series of earthworks located near the confluence of the Tallahatchie and Yalobusha. The Rebel forces, led by William Loring, had obstructed the rivers, and with heavy artillery fought the gunboats to a standstill March 11–16, 1863. Fearful of being trapped by obstructions in their rear, the gunboat commanders finally retreated, and the Confederates had another triumph.

Grant now tried yet another canal project. The Duckport Canal was intended to connect several Louisiana bayous west and south-west of Vicksburg and to empty into the Mississippi below the city. The idea continued Grant's long string of failures.

Still, he kept on. David Porter, who now commanded the naval fleet at Vicksburg, led a detachment of boats up Deer Creek via Steele's and Black bayous north of Vicksburg. The creek emptied into the Sunflower River, which in turn flowed into the Yazoo. Success would give Porter the option of going downriver to land near Vicksburg or upriver to attack Fort Pemberton from the south. Flood conditions and Confederate obstructions in the waterways almost trapped Porter; only timely rescue by Sherman's infantry saved the day. Porter escaped back to the Mississippi.

Thus far, all Union efforts to take Vicksburg and open the Mississippi had failed. Grant, however, could point to some underlying achievements. His campaign thus far had kept John Pemberton continually guessing as to the ultimate Federal intent. Grant's various ideas had Union troops marching all over the map, and Pemberton, not an overly confident officer anyway, was understandably confused. Perhaps sensing this, Grant decided to implement two diversions while he made a major move.

On March 29, Grant decided to send a large body of troops south down the Louisiana side of the Mississippi. He planned to send troop transports, and gunboats to protect them, steaming past the Vicksburg batteries to meet the detachment below and ferry them across the river. The batteries could be safely run; Farragut had proved that. Once out of harm's way, the vessels could travel down and ferry the troops across into Mississippi. Then Grant could launch a land campaign against Vicksburg. The Confederates, of course, could not be expected to sit idly by and do nothing; thus Grant had to divert their attention elsewhere.

In early April Grant sent Frederick Steele with a force to the Mississippi River town of Greenville. Steele moved inland along the upper reaches of Deer Creek, destroying Confederate property as he went. Steele's real mission was to make Pemberton think that Grant was still interested in operating along the waterways north of Vicksburg. The ruse worked. Pemberton became convinced that Grant was abandoning any idea of a direct assault on Vicksburg.

Steele's diversion paled in comparison to the success of a cavalry raid led by Colonel Benjamin Grierson. On April 17, Grierson led his large column of horsemen out of La Grange, Tennessee, into northeast Mississippi and followed the corridor between the Mississippi Central and the Mobile and Ohio railroads southward into central Mississippi. Grierson then turned southwest, arriving safely in Baton Rouge on May 2. Grierson adopted Grant's diversion tactics, sending out detachments from his main column. The result was massive frustration and confusion among Confederate cavalry trying to track Grierson's route.

Many small Mississippi towns and hamlets experienced their first war excitement when Grierson's riders came thundering through town. From the time they entered Mississippi until they escaped into Louisiana, the raiders rode through or near Ripley, Pontotoc, Houston, Starkville, Louisville, Philadelphia, Decatur, Newton Station (present-day Newton), Garlandville, Montrose, Raleigh, Westville, Hazlehurst, Byhalia, Union Church, Brookhaven, Summit (west of Summit a skirmish occurred at Wall's Bridge), Magnolia, and Osyka. Detachments of raiders also visited and/or fought skirmishes in such places as Palo Alto, Artesia, Macon, and Enterprise.

While Grierson rode, other Federal cavalry units scattered across north Mississippi, creating further consternation at Pemberton's headquarters. Pemberton grew so frustrated, and became so preoccupied with Grierson, that he even sent infantry east from Jackson to try and stop the Yankee horsemen.

On April 16, Union barges and transports began running the gauntlet of Confederate batteries at Vicksburg. There were losses; on the night of April 22, one transport and six barges were sunk by

Visitor Center, Grand Gulf State Park. Photo: Michael B. Ballard

Rebel gunners, but Grant soon had enough vessels safely downriver to ferry his troops across the river into Mississippi.

While worrying about Grierson and curious about the river activity, John Pemberton nevertheless had convinced himself that Grant had abandoned the idea of taking Vicksburg. So deluded had Pemberton become that he began offering troops to other theaters of the war. His superiors, not optimistic, discouraged him from sending troops anywhere just yet. Pemberton slowly began to see the light when reports started pouring in from his scouts and from John Bowen (commanding the garrison at Grand Gulf) that Union infantry, identified as John McClernand's corps, had been spotted moving down the Louisiana side of the river. Despite this awakening, Pemberton continued to worry more about Grierson than about all the Union activity much closer to Vicksburg. Then, while Grierson was escaping into Louisiana, Sherman demonstrated at Snyder's

Bluff on the Yazoo north of Vicksburg. Though not much of a demonstration, it was yet another of Grant's brilliant diversions that turned Pemberton's attention away from the real threat.

To the south on April 29, Union gunboats opened a tremendous barrage against the Rebel batteries at Grand Gulf. Grant had ideas of beating the batteries into submission and ferrying his troops across the river at the captured landing (as the result of floods and a disastrous fire, Grand Gulf had virtually ceased to exist as a town by April 1863). But the eight large cannon in forts Cobun and Wade held their own while inflicting considerable damage on three of Porter's boats. Grant had no choice but to go farther to find a crossing.

He decided on Bruinsburg, a river community connected by road to Port Gibson. Grant saw Port Gibson, located a few miles inland and almost due south of Vicksburg, as a potential site for gathering his army and making dispositions for his inland campaign. So the transfer of troops across the river began on April 30. It was the largest amphibious operation in military history up to that point.

John Bowen quickly tried to gather an army to contest Grant. Bowen had warned Pemberton right up to the last that reinforcements were desperately needed in the Port Gibson area. A few had been sent, but not nearly enough. Pemberton's self-delusion, plus his preoccupation with Grierson and Sherman, had cost him dearly. He had waited too long to make a decisive move. Now it was too late.

FIVE

Grant Triumphant: Vicksburg, Final Campaign and Siege

The steady tramp of Union infantry and the clatter of artillery drifted through the steep ravines and across the high ridges west of Port Gibson. On they came, their path lit by moonlight filtering through the moss and leaves of large hardwood trees. These were the men of John McClernand's XIII Corps, who had marched inland and then had turned right off the main road to Port Gibson. En route they had passed the magnificent mansion called Windsor, its giant columns casting eery shadows across the landscape. Union commanders feared that the road might be blocked up ahead. Scouts had found a connection from the main route to the Rodney-Port Gibson road, which ran parallel a few hundred yards to the south. So the men marched, urged on by McClernand, who feared that the Rebels, surely knowing by now of the landing at Bruinsburg, would burn bridges across Bayou Pierre near Port Gibson before the Yankees could do anything about it.

A desperate John Bowen was spending a hectic evening on the night of April 30–May 1, 1863. More than any other Confederate commander, Bowen had correctly guessed Grant's intentions, and he knew that if the Federals got a foothold in Mississippi there were not enough Confederate troops in the Port Gibson-Grand Gulf area to prevent an inland invasion. His only hope was to fight and beat Grant now and drive him back into the river.

While he looked anxiously for help from Vicksburg, Bowen sent troops under Martin Green hurrying to Port Gibson to block roads from the Mississippi leading into the town. Bowen's scouts had reported the false news that Union troops were streaming down both the Rodney and Bruinsburg roads. Green steered his troops onto the Rodney route, while a recently arrived brigade commanded by Edward Tracy marched down the Bruinsburg road. Bowen got word that William Baldwin's brigade should arrive from Vicksburg in time for the fight.

Martin Green, who had served under Sterling Price, spread his troops along a good defensive position at Magnolia Church. Just beyond sat the modest dwelling of A. K. Shaifer. Shaifer was not home, but his wife and other members of the household were warned that they were in harm's way. Having suddenly become fugitives, they quickly hitched horse to wagon and started furiously toward Port Gibson, just as the first Yankee bullets of the Battle of Port Gibson struck the side of the house. Green must have felt a bit embarrassed by the Shaifers' close call; he had just reassured them that the enemy was not nearby.

Although the real battle would not get under way until daylight, the opposing forces skirmished heavily in the darkness, a rare sight in a Civil War battle. When dawn came, Union commanders stood in amazement at the rugged terrain. Cane-choked hollows, a jigsaw puzzle of ravines, and narrow ridges would make coordinated attacks difficult at best. Also, word came from scouts that Tracy's brigade was approaching the Shaifer house by a small lane nearby that connected the Rodney and Bruinsburg roads. To meet this threat, McClernand sent a division led by Peter Osterhaus, an experienced Prussian officer who had settled in Missouri before the war.

Edward Tracy found himself in a quandary. Osterhaus's division suddenly appeared on his front, while at the same time he received an urgent appeal to send reinforcements to Green. The situation got further confused when Tracy died instantly from a sharpshooter's bullet. A colonel, Isham Garrott, took command and was ordered by Green to hold the Bruinsburg road at all costs. Green, meanwhile,

Schaifer House on Port Gibson Battlefield. Where first shots of the battle were fired. Photo: Michael B. Ballard

had been driven from his position at Magnolia Church back several hundred yards into the Willow Creek bottom. Victorious Union divisions commanded by Eugene Carr and A. P. Hovey rushed forward, their cheers echoing across the hollows.

Now William Baldwin's brigade arrived and tried to salvage the Confederate left, which had been smashed by Hovey and Carr. Baldwin stationed his men in a formidable defensive position amid the Willow Creek bottom, the two creek branches, and surrounding ridges. Colonel Francis Cockrell of Missouri appeared with his Grand Gulf troops and moved into position to support Baldwin. Martin Green, retreating beyond Baldwin to the Bruinsburg road, assumed command in that sector but, faced by Osterhaus's overwhelming numbers, had to retreat.

Though the bluecoats had won on their left, there was hard fighting yet over on the right. With excellent cover in the creek bottom, Baldwin's men held up McClernand's divisions for several hours. Cockrell's troops swung over to the far Confederate left to protect that flank and mauled James Slack's brigade. However, superior Union artillery and numbers eventually forced another Confederate retreat.

Bowen ordered his men to evacuate Port Gibson and to burn the bridges of Bayou Pierre behind them. Bowen had fought a remarkable fight considering that he was outnumbered by some twenty-four thousand to eight thousand. His hard-fighting soldiers had inflicted more casualties than they had received, but, in the end, simple numerical superiority made the difference. Bowen had given his commander, John Pemberton, more time to consolidate his command. Whether this would be enough to stop Grant remained to be seen.

Grant had a moment's hesitation about where to go from Port Gibson. He thought about moving south to link with Nathaniel Banks for joint operations against Port Hudson. Once that river fortress fell, the two armies could move north and take Vicksburg. But Banks had been delayed in getting to Port Hudson, and, rather than spend idle days waiting, Grant decided to move north and east, feeling his way toward Vicksburg.

Pemberton meanwhile had wanted to give up Port Hudson altogether and concentrate everything he had on defending Vicksburg. In fact reinforcements for Pemberton from Franklin Gardner, Confederate commander at Port Hudson, were already en route. Jefferson Davis had other ideas. Davis wired Pemberton that holding both Port Hudson and Vicksburg was necessary to maintain contact with the Transmississippi. Pemberton notified Gardner, who managed ultimately to scrape together some seven thousand men to fight Banks and to hold him at bay until after Vicksburg had fallen. Pemberton would certainly have need of those troops in the coming weeks.

While his opponent struggled to consolidate, Grant marched his

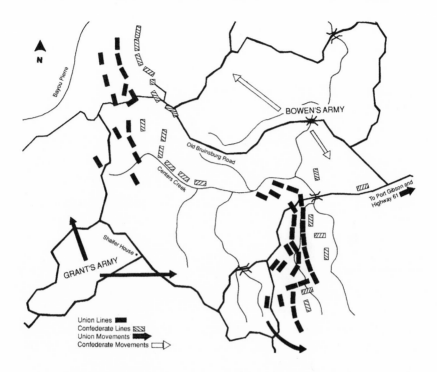

Battle of Port Gibson, May 1, 1863 (Note: Current roads on the battlefield do not always follow 1863 routes.)

men toward the Southern Railroad, the vital supply line that connected Vicksburg with Jackson and points east. Grant had two of his three corps on hand: McClernand's XIII, which had done the bulk of the fighting at Port Gibson, and the XVII, led by the bright, popular James McPherson. Sherman and his XV corps were on the way. Once the entire force was on hand, Grant would have some forty-five thousand men. Pemberton could match him, but only if he abandoned many outlying areas, something he was hesitant to do, especially after President Davis's admonition to hold on to Port Hudson.

While his army moved, Grant established a supply depot at Grand

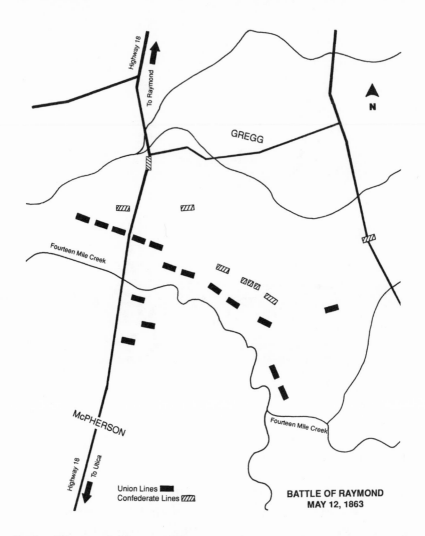

Battle of Raymond, May 12, 1863

Gulf. Supply wagons would follow the army into central Mississippi. Grant claimed after the war that he cut himself loose from his supply line, but he did not. The heavily laden wagons kept his men supplied until he reestablished contact with the river after investing Vicksburg.

While Grant's forces marched north by northeast, feinting toward the Big Black River, which cut a south-by-southwesterly course from a few miles east of Vicksburg to its mouth near Grand Gulf, Pemberton spread his troops along the west bank of the Big Black to keep an eye on the Yankees. The bluffs along the bank gave Pemberton an excellent defensive position, and if he remained firm Grant would have difficulty breaking through. But the indecisive Pemberton was surrounded by many officers making varied suggestions. His life would become even more complicated with the arrival of Joseph E. Johnston, Pemberton's immediate superior, a few days later. Johnston's ideas differed from Jefferson Davis's. Pemberton would be caught in the middle.

For the moment, Pemberton listened to William W. Loring, who firmly believed that he, not Pemberton, should be commanding the army. In the coming campaign, Loring did much to assure Confederate defeat. As the Federal columns marched north, he ignored a golden opportunity to strike McPherson's corps. The truth seemed to be that when push came to shove, Loring was no more a fighter than Pemberton. But he had plenty of counsel, and now he was advising Pemberton to send a detachment out to check on Grant, who, after all, might turn and attack Jackson first.

As fate would have it, a brigade led by John Gregg had just arrived by rail in Jackson. Gregg was on his way from Port Hudson to join Pemberton. Instead, Gregg got orders to march to Raymond, just a few miles west of Jackson. He was to report any sightings of soldiers in blue. On May 12, Gregg awoke to the news that Yankees had been spotted on the Utica-Raymond road south of town. Assuming that this was part of a screen for Grant's army, which was probably turn-

Hinds County Courthouse, Raymond, Mississippi. Used as a hospital during the Vicksburg Campaign. Photo: Michael B. Ballard

ing left to attack the railroad at Edwards near where the rail line crossed the Big Black, Gregg ordered what he thought would be a flank attack.

Gregg had no idea until it was too late that these Federals were the van of McPherson's entire corps. The Confederates attacked at Fourteen Mile Creek, and, although fighting impressively, were soon overwhelmed by McPherson's superior numbers. Gregg's men suffered only about seventy more casualties than McPherson's, largely because they streamed back into Jackson before things got out of hand. Gregg's poor decision to fight without knowing whom he was fighting had now cut him off from Pemberton.

Grant decided that the presence of Gregg and probably several thousand more Confederates at Jackson meant that he could not turn his back on the capital city and go after Pemberton. Word had come that Joseph Johnston was in Jackson now, and he just might assault the rear of Grant's army if it turned west. So Grant made the decision to attack Jackson, which he did on May 14. McClernand kept an eye on Pemberton while Grant's other two corps charged the Rebel works west and south of Jackson. Johnston offered little resistance, even though more Confederates were arriving almost hourly from the east. If Johnston had fought hard, Grant might have gotten bogged down, giving Pemberton a chance to move and attack the Union rear. But Johnston was no fighter. A bitter enemy of Jefferson Davis, he had come to Mississippi with a negative attitude and was ready to give up Vicksburg and abandon Mississippi to Grant.

Johnston withdrew to Canton, northeast of Jackson. Before leaving Jackson, he had sent word to Pemberton to link their commands at Clinton between Jackson and Vicksburg. Unfortunately for the Confederates, a Union spy got a copy of the message, and Grant hurried to fight Pemberton before the two Rebel commanders could join forces. He need not have been in too big a rush, for Pemberton was hesitating to do anything. He had contradictory orders to consider. Davis had said Vicksburg must be held; Johnston was giving an order that would make the city vulnerable to Grant. Pemberton called a council of war, and after much debate decided to move southeast from the Edwards area and attack Grant's supply line. That way he could stay between the Yankees and Vicksburg. Also, Pemberton figured that once he broke the supply line he could move north and join with Johnston. It was a strange sort of compromise between the directives of Davis and Johnston and would doubtless please neither. In Pemberton's defense, he did not know that Johnston had already abandoned Jackson.

Pemberton marched toward Raymond amid all sorts of difficulty. First he had to wait for an ammunition train from Vicksburg, and then his army had to find another marching route because the Bakers Creek crossing was flooding, something his scouts should have known and reported. On the night of May 15, his army camped

Joseph E. Johnston. Confederate general who played a key role in the Vicksburg Campaign. Credit: Ezra J. Warner, *Generals in Gray*, Baton Rouge: LSU Press

along an irregular line northwest to southeast from north of the Jackson-Vicksburg road over to the Raymond-Edwards road. Actually it was not a bad place to be. His left and center rested along the base of an eminence called Champion Hill. His right was on a ridge overlooking Jackson Creek bottom. He had no idea of fighting here despite campfires to the east that indicated a strong enemy presence. Pemberton did not warn his men to prepare for battle. He ignored the obvious evidence that the Yankees could be coming his way.

Early on the morning of May 16, Pemberton got Johnston's message from Canton announcing the fall of Jackson and reiterating a junction at Clinton. This time Pemberton chose not to hesitate. He ordered his army to reverse its route and move north, then east to Clinton. As the army prepared to move, the lead elements of Grant's army opened fire. McClernand's corps deployed on either side of

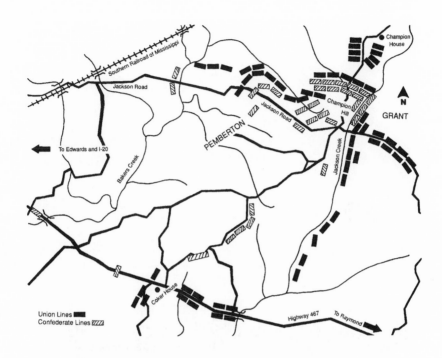

Battle of Champion Hill, May 16, 1863 (Note: Current roads around Champion Hill are different than in 1863.)

the Raymond road, the right moving toward the Middle Road, which ran between the Jackson and Raymond roads. McPherson's blue column marched down the Jackson road, spreading to the right and to the left toward the Middle Road. Pemberton had no choice but to fight.

The initial phase of the battle on the Confederate right was sporadic, with McClernand feeling his way rather than pushing an all-out charge. Loring opposed McClernand, putting up a decent defense (helped by McClernand's timidity) along the high ridge west

Coker House on Champion Hill Battlefield between Edwards and Raymond. Currently being restored by the Jackson, Mississippi, Civil War Round Table. Photo: Michael B. Ballard

of Jackson Creek. The turning points of the battle would be on the Confederate left and center.

On the left Carter Stevenson commanded, and his troops were savaged by the divisions of A. P. Hovey and John Logan, one of the war's best civilian soldiers. With his left crumbling, Pemberton began shifting troops in that direction. He met with some resistance from John Bowen, holding the Confederate center, and from Loring. Both feared that shifting troops to the left would weaken their parts of the line. But the left was the immediate priority, and finally Bowen rushed his men into the breach. Loring continued to refuse Pemberton's orders until it was too late.

Bowen's men staged one of the most spectacular charges of the war. Led by Francis Cockrell's Missourians, Bowen's division stormed Champion Hill, dubbed the "hill of death" by Hovey, and drove Hovey's brigades to the crest of the hill and beyond. But without help from Loring, and with Stevenson noticeably absent as his men tried to shore up the Confederate left, Bowen's men soon ran out of steam and yielded to reinforcements sent to the danger zone by Grant.

Finally, McClernand got into the act on the Union left, forcing Pemberton to stop transferring troops from his right. With increasing pressure all along the front, Pemberton had no choice but to order a retreat. Loring held off McClernand long enough for Bowen and Stevenson to get their divisions on the road to the Big Black. McPherson's tired troops did little to pressure the retreating Rebels. Once Grant did get his army moving forward, however, Loring got cut off from the retreat and had to swing his men south, then northeast, to the safety of the Union rear. Loring eventually led his division north to join Johnston.

During the decisive struggle at Champion Hill, Pemberton lost thirty-eight hundred of his twenty-three thousand, while Grant suffered twenty-four hundred casualties out of thirty-two thousand. Pemberton had made the mistake of leaving two divisions guarding Vicksburg. He could have left a much smaller garrison to guard the city's considerable defenses, while beefing up his field army. Had his numbers been equal to Grant's at Champion Hill, the outcome might well have been different.

None of that mattered now, as Pemberton's men streamed back to works on the east side of the Big Black. Pemberton waited longer than he should have, no doubt hoping that Loring somehow would be able to rejoin the army. The next day, May 17, Grant ordered an attack, and Pemberton's men, low on morale and still heavily outnumbered, retreated in a panic-stricken rout across the river. Troops stationed along the high bluff on the west bank managed to slow the Federal onslaught, and the Confederates burned the railroad bridge and a boat that had been used for a bridge. Thus thwarted, Grant called off immediate pursuit. Even if the Confederates beat him to Vicksburg, he still felt confident that the city was now his. Also,

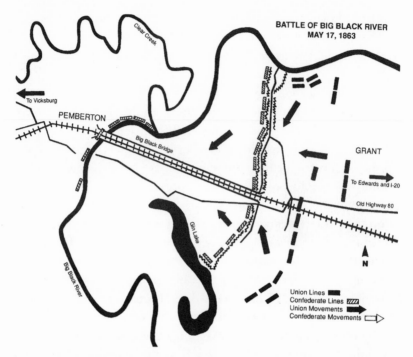

Battle of Big Black River, May 17, 1863

Grant perhaps thought that Pemberton would turn north rather than risk getting his army bottled up in Vicksburg.

Pemberton certainly had the option of escaping, but apparently such a move never crossed his mind. He rode sadly to Bovina along with his troops before catching the train back into fortress Vicksburg. He was determined to follow Davis's dictum to hold on to the town. He would later write that he considered Vicksburg "the most important point in the Confederacy." A note from Johnston ordered Pemberton to save the army by evacuating the city's fortifications, but by the time it arrived Grant's artillery was shelling the city. Union cannon gave Pemberton the excuse he needed to stay right where he was.

Visitor Center, Vicksburg National Military Park. Photo: Michael B. Ballard

In Vicksburg, Pemberton placed Stevenson's wrecked division on the far right of the Confederate line, the area least likely to be immediately attacked by Grant. He put the two fresh divisions that had remained in Vicksburg, John Forney's and Martin L. Smith's, in the center and on the left respectively. Bowen's proud division was held in reserve behind the left center of the line.

Underestimating both the strength of the Confederate works and the resolve of Pemberton's men, Grant ordered two assaults on May 19 and May 22, both dismal failures. McClernand attacked down the Baldwin's Ferry road on the Union left, McPherson in the center along the Jackson road, and William T. Sherman, who had missed Champion Hill and Big Black due to mopping-up operations in Jackson, sent his rested troops down Graveyard Road on the Union right. Sherman's men especially suffered as they ran into the Confederate bulwark known as Stockade Redan. McClernand made some progress against the Railroad Redoubt in his front on May 22, but all

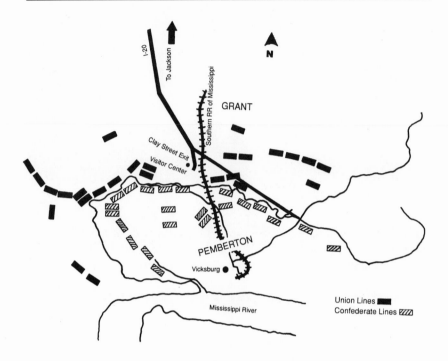

Siege of Vicksburg, May 19-July 4, 1863

he earned was dismissal from Grant when the political general later published a newspaper article proclaiming glory for his corps at the expense of the rest of the army. McClernand's sin was in fact rather minor, but Grant was looking for any excuse to send the troublesome general home.

Giving up on assault strategy, Grant settled for siege tactics. For forty-seven days his forces bombarded Vicksburg, all the while digging trenches bringing them ever closer to the Confederate lines. His heavy artillery made life miserable for Pemberton's army and for the civilians still in Vicksburg. Meanwhile, Grant kept an eye out toward the Big Black in case Joseph Johnston made a move to relieve Pemberton. He also sent an expedition up the Yazoo to destroy the

John C. Pemberton's headquarters during the siege of Vicksburg. Privately owned and currently undergoing renovation. Photo: Michael B. Ballard

Yazoo City shipyard that had produced the *Arkansas*. Federal patrols destroyed food and other supplies in the Mechanicsburg corridor, the area northeast of Vicksburg between the Yazoo and the Big Black, to prevent Joseph Johnston or anybody else from taking that route to rescue the Vicksburg garrison. All these activities increased Pemberton's isolation.

Pemberton was far more anxious than Grant, because he soon realized that Johnston was his only hope. But Johnston delayed and delayed, complaining to Richmond that he did not have enough men and supplies. His correspondence with Pemberton was sporadic at best, given the Union noose that was ever tightening around Vicksburg. The two Confederates discussed where Johnston should attack, and how Pemberton might break out, but in the end Johnston did nothing, leaving Pemberton to his own devices. As for Pemberton, he could do little more than reduce rations daily, trying to stretch his supplies to extend the siege long enough for help to arrive.

Vicksburg and its occupants suffered severely as the siege dragged on through hot, dry weather. Citizens mostly dwelt in caves, coming out to check their homes only during lulls in the shelling. Physicians and nurses had to cope with terrible hospital conditions, made worse when occasionally a Union shell would drop in their midst, further wounding or killing the wounded. Sickness became a severe problem because of water shortages and undernourishment.

As the siege crept into late June, Grant's engineers dug underground and exploded mines, severely damaging Confederate works at the Third Louisiana Redan. The mining operations revealed how vulnerable Pemberton's lines had become.

As July dawned, Pemberton knew it was time for a decision. He polled his generals to see how they felt about breaking out, perhaps to the south where the Union lines seemed most vulnerable. All the officers rejected the idea. The men were in no condition to fight their way through, and, even if they could, artillery would have to be left behind because of the absence of horses and the soldiers' weakened physical condition. And the troops would have to travel between the Mississippi and the Big Black, where they might be shelled by Union gunboats.

Faced with such stark realities, Pemberton contacted Grant about surrender terms. Initially demanding unconditional surrender, Grant accepted less when he saw that Pemberton would not hesitate to keep on fighting unless some modifications were added. The two commanders turned the negotiations over to their subordinates and, late on July 3, a final deal was struck. Pemberton's men would be paroled (promising not to fight until exchanged for Union prisoners on a one-to-one basis) rather than sent to prison camps. Pemberton and his officers could retain their side arms, clothing, and a

Old Courthouse Museum, Vicksburg. Was the Warren County Courthouse during the war. Photo: Michael B. Ballard

horse each. The formal surrender came on July 4, and southerners never forgave Pemberton for surrendering on that date. Pemberton later insisted that he did so in order to get better surrender terms.

The Vicksburg campaign was far-reaching in its results. Pemberton had surrendered an entire army, almost thirty thousand men, as well as large quantities of artillery and ammunition. The loss of Vicksburg forced the surrender of Port Hudson. The Confederacy was now divided, the Mississippi being totally controlled by the Union navy. More great victories lay ahead for Grant, who would eventually be named general of all Union armies. Pemberton would never command an army again. In 1864 he resigned his generalship and accepted a lieutenant colonelcy of artillery. Many of his soldiers were furloughed and never returned to the army.

The war would drag on for two more years. It was being decided in the west, where Confederate resistance had been gradually crumbling ever since the losses of forts Henry and Donelson. But Vicksburg was the key turning point, because the Confederacy had lost far more than it could ever hope to regain.

SUGGESTIONS FOR FURTHER READING

Ballard, Michael B. *Pemberton: A Biography.* Jackson: University Press of Mississippi, 1991.

Bearss, Edwin C. *Rebel Victory at Vicksburg.* Vicksburg, MS: Vicksburg Centennial Commemoration Commission, 1963.

———. *The Vicksburg Campaign.* 3 vols. Dayton, OH: Morningside, 1985–86.

Brown, D. Alexander. *Grierson's Raid: A Cavalry Adventure of the Civil War.* Urbana: University of Illinois Press, 1962. Reprint.

Grant, U. S. *Personal Memoirs of U. S. Grant.* New York: AMS Press, 1972. Reprint.

Hoehling, A. A. *Vicksburg: 47 Days of Siege.* Mechanicsburg, PA: Stackpole Books, 1996. Reprint.

Miers, Earl S. *The Web of Victory: Grant at Vicksburg.* New York: Knopf, 1955.

Symonds, Craig L. *Joseph E. Johnston: A Civil War Biography.* New York: W. W. Norton and Company, 1992.

PART III
Meridian, Brice's Cross Roads, and Tupelo

In the aftermath of the Vicksburg campaign, William T. Sherman
went east, besieged Joseph Johnston at Jackson, soon forcing him to
the Mississippi hinterland. Johnston had marched his men to the Big
Black, but had arrived there only in time to hear of Vicksburg's surrender. Sherman wanted not only to chase Johnston away but "to go
on eastward and destroy the remaining railroads of the State in and
near Meridian." Supply depots at Meridian had kept Vicksburg supplied and were still supplying large areas of Mississippi and Alabama.

Sherman decided to wait. As he wrote a few months afterward,
"The period of the year [summer], the intense heat and drought,
and the condition of our men after the long siege of Vicksburg ren-
dered the accomplishment of the plan then impracticable, and it
had to be deferred to a later period." As things turned out, the de-
ferment lasted longer than Sherman had planned. The defeat of
William Rosecrans by Braxton Bragg at Chickamauga in September
of 1863 forced U. S. Grant to send much of the Vicksburg army, including Sherman, to Chattanooga, where Rosecrans had been bottled up by Bragg. Finally, Grant defeated Bragg, and Sherman returned to Vicksburg where his main job was to secure the victory
there by destroying Confederate war-making capabilities on either
side of the Mississippi for several miles inland. The Meridian campaign of early 1864 would be a part of that strategy.

Later that same year Sherman would return to Georgia and lead a
group of Union armies from Chattanooga toward Atlanta. During

that campaign he grew anxious about the raiding capabilities of Nathan Bedford Forrest, who had put a damper on the Meridian campaign by defeating a large Union cavalry force. To keep Forrest tied down in Mississippi and away from his ever-lengthening supply line back to and through Chattanooga to Nashville, Sherman ordered an expedition to fight, and attempt to eliminate, the intrepid cavalryman. The result was a Forrest victory at Brice's Cross Roads. Sherman then ordered another operation, which resulted in Union victory at Tupelo. These two north Mississippi campaigns marked the end of major campaigning in the state.

SIX

Securing a Victory:
The Meridian Campaign

William T. Sherman had reason to be confident. He knew that the Confederate commander in Mississippi, Leonidas Polk, did not have enough men to successfully contest the movement of Union troops in Mississippi. Because Polk's troops were scattered over a wide area, all Sherman really had to do was order a few feints here and there, and the Rebel troops would remain scattered and relatively impotent.

So Sherman organized the Meridian campaign. His purpose was "to break up the enemy's railroads at and about Meridian, and to do the enemy as much damage as possible in the month of February [1864], and to be prepared by the 1st of March to assist General [Nathaniel] Banks in a similar dash at the Red River country, especially Shreveport [Louisiana], the whole to result in widening our domain along the Mississippi River, and thereby set the troops hitherto necessary to guard the river free for other military purposes."

Sherman's plan included having General William Sooy Smith bring a large force of cavalry from Memphis southeast through Mississippi to Meridian. Smith received orders to arrive in Meridian by February 10. His ride to Meridian was not to be encumbered by "minor objects"; instead he was to concentrate on destroying bridges, railroads, and "corn not wanted." While Smith's horsemen made their way from Memphis, Sherman would be leading divisions from Stephen Hurlbut's XVI and James McPherson's XVII army corps on a direct line from Vicksburg to Meridian. Hurlbut had been in command at Memphis during the Vicksburg campaign. Once the forces joined up at Meridian and the proper destruction around that town was achieved, Sherman would then make decisions about any further operations.

Sherman also ordered an operation along the Yazoo River, and, before the Federal columns reached Meridian, ordered enough feinting to convince Polk that an attack on Mobile, Alabama, was eminent. Troops from Mobile that might have retarded Sherman's march rushed back to that Gulf Coast city. Polk's other forces remained scattered as the Confederates tried to remain flexible enough to counter any unexpected Union attacks. But the lack of Confederate concentration only made Sherman's task that much easier.

To counter this Yankee thrust, Stephen D. Lee, a Vicksburg veteran now in command of cavalry in Mississippi, had but three brigades of horsemen readily available. Lawrence S. Ross's Texas brigade patrolled the Yazoo River area, while trying to keep an eye on the Mississippi Central Railroad. Ross would be confronting the Federal Yazoo operation. Peter B. Starke's cavalry brigade was stationed at Brownsville near the Big Black just north of Edwards to watch the river crossings. Wirt Adams's brigade rode from Natchez to the Raymond area. The horsemen of Adams's and Starke's brigades would be involved in almost constant skirmishing with Sherman's army in the coming campaign.

On February 3, 1864, the Union march from Vicksburg to Meridian began. Cavalry moved east and secured the bridge across Bakers Creek on the Champion Hill battlefield. The main body of troops camped near Edwards. The next morning the Union columns started toward Clinton. Confederate cavalry kept up a continual harassment, but were easily pushed back. A counterattack by Federal horsemen drove the Rebels beyond Bolton. Here the Confederates dug in on the east side of a creek and were reinforced during the night.

On the morning of February 5, two of McPherson's brigades advanced, and several pieces of Union artillery pounded the Confederate position. The Rebels quickly gave way under the pressure of the Yankee advance, and the main body of Sherman's army marched unchecked through Clinton. Union cavalry swung south and then north, just missing the flank of the retreating Confederates.

At Clinton, Sherman issued the kind of order that kept the enemy guessing. McPherson took his divisions south so that he would approach Jackson from a direction (southwest to northeast) different from the one taken by Hurlbut's men, who continued from Clinton on a due east route. Union cavalry meanwhile pressed the retreating Confederates in an effort to beat them into Jackson if possible to keep the Rebels from destroying the Pearl River bridge. The Confederates managed to cut loose a pontoon bridge that came apart in the river, but the Federal horsemen dashed into the Pearl and rescued the pontoon materials. Federal infantry swung north toward Canton to see if the rumored Confederate infantry of William Loring and Samuel French were marching to Jackson. The threat never materialized.

The next day, February 6, Union engineers put together the pontoon bridge, and the army began crossing the Pearl late that afternoon. The following morning blue columns entered Brandon, camping just east of town. That evening Union cavalry that had been left to guard the rear in Jackson arrived and prepared to take the lead on February 8 as the army again marched eastward.

Skirmishing between the Federal advance and Confederate cavalry continued all day. Sherman's force camped the night of the eighth about four miles from Morton along Line Creek. Again Union scouts reported the presence of Loring's and French's combined infantry to the east, but reconnaissance showed that if the Rebel commanders had been disposed to make a stand, they had changed their minds and had withdrawn.

On February 9, the army entered Morton and spent hours tearing up railroad track, employing the usual method of burning crossties to heat the rails and then bending those to make them useless (such rails came to be called "Sherman's bowties"). The XVI Corps took the advance; the next day the army reached within a few miles of Hillsboro, the county seat of Scott County. After leaving the Hillsboro area on February 11, the march began to bog down in difficult, swampy terrain.

At Lake Station on the eleventh, the Yankees wrought significant damage, destroying "the railroad buildings, machine-shops, turning-table, several cars, and one locomotive." Minor cavalry skirmishing occurred, but the blue columns kept moving, reaching Decatur late on the afternoon of February 12 and Tallahatta Creek the next day. At Decatur, some of Stephen Lee's cavalry hit the Union flank and disabled several wagons but had to leave the wagons behind because of "the proximity of the [enemy's] infantry."

On February 14 as the main column moved ahead, a detachment was sent south to destroy railroad bridges and equipment at Chunky Station. En route to Chunky the detachment made contact with the rear guard of Confederate Wirt Adams's cavalry, which still shadowed and occasionally skirmished with Sherman's scouts. Adams lost a few wagons during this brief fight. The main column meanwhile camped within four miles of Meridian.

On February 15, the Union advance at last entered Meridian, and for the next five days soldiers scattered about in various detachments, destroying most of Meridian as well as track and equipment in four directions. Sherman wrote in his campaign report, "10,000 men worked hard and with a will in that work of destruction, with axes, crowbars, sledges, clawbars, and with fire, and I have no hesitation in pronouncing the work as well done. Meridian, with its depots, store-houses, arsenal, hospitals, offices, hotels, and cantonments no longer exists."

Sherman ordered Hurlbut to supervise destruction north and east of Meridian, while McPherson was assigned sectors south and

William Sooy Smith.
Union cavalry comman-
der routed by Nathan
Bedford Forrest during
the Meridian Campaign.
Credit: Ezra J. Warner,
Generals in Blue, Baton
Rouge: LSU Press

west of town. Their soldiers combined to destroy nearly 120 miles of track. McPherson's men ventured south through Enterprise and Quitman, tearing up thousands of feet of trestles as well as bridges and equipment along the way. Sherman noted triumphantly that the rail line from Jackson to Meridian had been destroyed and that the destruction continued in all directions from the once formidable Confederate depot at the latter.

One thing had gone wrong for the Federal army during the campaign: Sooy Smith and his cavalry had not showed up. Sherman wanted Smith on hand to lead the march back to Vicksburg. Smith had a force sufficient to brush aside Confederate cavalry that might be encountered along the way. Sherman was concerned that additional gray riders might have gathered in his rear ready to contest the return march. Sherman waited in vain for Smith until February 20, when he ordered a return to Vicksburg.

McPherson's troops followed the main road back, while Sherman traveled with Hurlbut on a route slightly north of McPherson. Sherman ordered Hurlbut to send out a cavalry detachment to the north to see if any contact could be made with Smith. If Smith could not be found, scouts were to be sent to him with orders that he meet Sherman's army at Canton. Hurlbut's column made its way through Union, while riders ranged as far north as Philadelphia and Louisville in search of Smith. McPherson meanwhile veered slightly north as he marched back through Decatur and Hillsboro where the two columns merged. Sherman led his army north of Jackson on to Canton and Brownsville, finally reaching its old camps between the Big Black and Vicksburg on March 4. Smith did not show up at Canton; Sherman would soon be infuriated when he found out what had happened to his absent cavalry commander.

William Sooy Smith had had trouble getting his column under way from Memphis. He blamed bad roads, flood conditions, and myriad other factors for all the delays that kept him from setting his column in motion until February 11, the day after Sherman had expected him to be in Meridian. Finally under way, Smith kept a wary eye out for Nathan Bedford Forrest, who reportedly had his cavalry strung out along the south side of the Tallahatchie River.

The cavalry column rode through Wyatt, protected on the flank by infantry sent out by Smith to help meet Forrest if the fiery Confederate was indeed waiting at the Tallahatchie. Smith feinted crossing at Wyatt while swinging his column over to New Albany. He moved rapidly on through Pontotoc to Houston, where Mississippi state troops resisted the invaders in a swampy area, thereby slowing Smith's march. Again he maneuvered away from trouble, ordering his advance to fight the small Rebel contingent at Houston while he moved the main column to Okolona. There his men surprised and captured several Confederates, including a few officers and men on furlough.

From Okolona, Smith sent a detachment to check for a possible crossing of the Tombigbee River at Aberdeen. Apparently Smith had in his mind getting away from any resistance by moving into Alabama and riding southward to Meridian. Another regiment was sent to Aberdeen as support and also to scout for Confederate forces in the direction of Columbus. Two other regiments rode south from Okolona along the Mobile and Ohio Railroad toward West Point to check for the enemy along crossings of the Sakatonchee Creek. Smith gave orders to destroy Confederate supplies, and the West Point riders tore up track as they went. Smith soon got reports that Confederates seemed to gathering in force south of West Point.

Bedford Forrest's scouts had kept him well informed of Smith's route. Forrest quickly decided that Smith must be on his way to join Sherman, so he began calling in his widely scattered force for a concentration at Starkville, a few miles southwest of West Point. Forrest also guessed correctly that Smith might have an eye on crossing the Tombigbee, so he sent a brigade to Columbus to block that route. Another brigade rode in the direction of Aberdeen to check on possible Federal activity. Forrest wanted to know exactly what Smith was up to before acting in force.

On the morning of February 20, Forrest's brother, Colonel Jeffrey Forrest, who was leading the Aberdeen expedition, ran into Smith's cavalry and fell back toward West Point. The fighting spread, and General Forrest rushed assistance to the front, which moved to within three miles north of West Point. Finding that Smith's column was "in heavy force," Forrest ordered a retreat to find ground of his own choosing on which to fight. News that Stephen Lee had ordered reinforcements to the West Point area lifted Forrest's spirits. An instinctive soldier, Forrest made the shrewd move of pulling his men behind Sakatonchee Creek southwest of West Point on the Starkville road. Smith would have to fight him here, turn back, or move on southeast with Forrest in his rear. Certainly Smith could not continue toward Meridian, so he would have to pick one of the first two options. To further confuse Smith, Forrest left a few men south of

West Point and sent a detachment north up the Sakatonchee to counter a crossing by one of Smith's detachments.

Smith got spooked; in his report he cited a litany of reasons why he suddenly decided to retreat. The Confederates were concentrating against him on all fronts. Several thousand slaves had taken "refuge" in the Union ranks; this encumbered his ability to maneuver his troops. He had to protect his pack mules; such a duty tied down a large part of his force. The enemy was better armed for dismounted fighting than his men (not many Union officers ever made such a claim!). He had confidence in the fighting ability of only one brigade; the rest of the troops were undisciplined. He was already so late getting to Meridian that Sherman had probably given up on him. His men had destroyed much cotton and corn and railroad track already. So Smith's excuses went for the withdrawal he was about to order. The truth was that he had simply lost his nerve.

On February 21 Smith did order an advance on Forrest's main position along the Ellis Bridge crossing of the Sakatonchee about three miles from West Point. From Smith's campaign report, one would never know a fight took place there, but Forrest wrote of the battle in which Federal troops attacked Jeffrey Forrest's position. Bedford's brother had ordered breastworks of rails thrown up, and the fire of his men from this protection inflicted considerable casualties during a two-hour fight. No doubt Smith considered this only a holding action. The rest of his column was withdrawing.

Forrest, meanwhile, had ordered troopers to fan out on Smith's flanks and rear and to cause as much trouble as possible. Smith soon had his whole column pulling back to Okolona, so as, he said, to draw the enemy out and make them fight on ground of his choosing. This was a retreat, however, not tactical maneuvers to find a better place to fight. Skirmishing, heavy at times, marked the route of Smith's retreat. The Federals passed through and beyond Okolona, where they made a short-lived stand, swinging now onto the Pontotoc road. Forrest hurried his men along, pushing the attack.

At a place called Ivey's Farm, Smith found a nice long ridge conducive to defense and decided to make another stand. Sharp fighting took place there as the Confederates continued to press on. Jeffrey Forrest fell dead during the action. His brother Bedford rode up, dismounted, and briefly cradled his younger brother's head in his arms. Bedford then arose and had the fiery look in his eye that his men had come to recognize and respect. They knew that Smith's men were in for it now, for when Forrest got that look there was no holding him back.

He personally led the charge that chased Smith's men from their well-chosen position. When Smith made one last effort to stem Forrest's pursuit about ten miles from Pontotoc, Forrest chose a few men and again personally led the charge that sent the Yankees flying. By now the pursuing Rebels were exhausted, and Forrest, satisfied that he had punished Smith as much as he could, ordered a halt. A grateful Smith hurried his force on back to Memphis. All his explanations for his failure fell on deaf ears at Sherman's headquarters. Sherman was furious, and Smith resigned several weeks later, reportedly because of ill health. (Smith enjoyed a successful postwar career as an engineer.)

The other major aspect of Sherman's Meridian campaign in Mississippi went somewhat better for the Union cause. Sherman's major purpose in ordering an expedition up the Yazoo River was to convince the planters in the region along the river that the war for them was over and that they should stop giving aid and comfort to Confederate soldiers. The trip up the Yazoo would convince Rebel sympathizers that the Union controlled that river and could inflict punishment at any time. If the river column found any who resisted allegiance to the Union, property was to be destroyed accordingly.

The Federal force, commanded by James Coates, embarked on transports from the mouth of the Yazoo on February 1. The small contingent included black Union soldiers of the Eighth Louisiana (U.S.) regiment. Other black soldiers of the First Mississippi (U.S.)

cavalry joined the expedition at Hayne's Bluff overlooking the Yazoo north of Vicksburg.

During the course of the trip upriver, Coates ordered two stops in the Satartia area to look for reported Confederates. A few scattered shots were exchanged and some Confederate artillery shells made life interesting for the Federals, but the Yankees did not encounter serious resistance until they were within a couple of miles of a place called Liverpool, where a portion of Lawrence Ross's Texas cavalry brigade shelled the bluecoats with two pieces of artillery. Coates disembarked his men and confronted the Texans, who put up a stiff resistance behind their breastworks. They had anticipated action here because they knew obstructions in the river would force the Union vessels to slow, making them better artillery targets. Federal gunboats accompanying the expedition came up to shell the Rebel guns.

The battle at Liverpool on February 3 was a tactical victory for Ross. Coates's men could not penetrate the Confederate line and had to retreat. So fierce had been the Texans' resistance that Coates became convinced he was heavily outnumbered. His men reboarded the transports and the Federal fleet retreated downriver for the night. The next day, the Union boats again came up, and Ross, running low on ammunition, had no choice but to let them go by. He ordered his men on to Yazoo City.

Ross won the race to Yazoo City and posted his men. The Confederates were waiting when advance Union gunboats came into view on February 5. Ross's rifled cannon disabled one gunboat, and the rest fell back beyond the range of his guns and tossed shells into the town. Coates, intimidated by his Liverpool brush with Ross, held his infantry back and did not take possession of Yazoo City until February 9. By then Ross and his Texans had gone to Benton to await further orders, which sent them to assist Confederate resistance against Sherman's Meridian columns. They later rode north to Starkville to help Forrest, who by the time they arrived had already driven Smith away. Ross and his hard-riding cavalry almost participated in all three aspects of the Meridian campaign.

From Yazoo City, Coates and his column proceeded as far upriver as Greenwood, arriving there February 14, where they found Fort Pemberton evacuated. While there, he sent a cavalry detachment toward Grenada, where they encountered heavy resistance reportedly from Forrest and his cavalry. The report was not true, but Coates was probably relieved when he received orders to return to Yazoo City and hold the town until further notice. He took his time going back downriver, as he followed Sherman's instructions to wreak havoc on the "plantations of disloyal parties." A few miles above Yazoo City, Coates disembarked his whole cavalry force to check all the roads around the town.

Some of Coates's black riders reconnoitering the road to Benton ran headlong into Ross's Texans, who had arrived back from their Starkville trek. Ross ordered a charge, and later reported that the "road all the way to Yazoo City was literally strewed with their bodies." Coates admitted that his loss in this fight "was rather heavy."

Coates's men occupied Yazoo City and built defensive works. Parts of Yazoo City took on the look of Vicksburg during the siege, though on a much smaller scale. Ross bided his time until he was reinforced on March 4. The next day the Confederates attacked. Fighting raged in the streets of Yazoo City as the heavily pressed Federals ran for their redoubts. Ross demanded the surrender of one redoubt but was refused. The Confederates concentrated their artillery and pounded the Union positions. Meanwhile, cotton captured by the Yankees, as well as storehouses of Union supplies, burned at the touch of Rebel torches. Finally, Ross decided that his force had done all it could, and he ordered a retreat, which he said was accomplished "quietly and without confusion." Coates insisted that the Rebels retreated in a rout due to his effective countercharges.

Whatever the case, the battle for Yazoo City was over. Union reinforcements forced Ross to retreat to Benton. And Coates soon received orders to bring his column back to Vicksburg. The Meridian campaign was finally over.

As for the victorious William T. Sherman, his shadow would continue over Mississippi for several more months. Sherman sent part of his Meridian force to join Nathaniel Banks's expedition up the Red River in Louisiana. Sherman left for Chattanooga and the command of an army group assigned to invade Georgia and capture Atlanta. As he marched into Georgia, he would be looking over his shoulder toward his shaky supply line. He especially worried that one Nathan Bedford Forrest might destroy the vital rail lines in his rear. So he issued orders to make sure that Forrest was kept busy in Mississippi.

SEVEN

The Wizard's Magic:
The Battle of Brice's Cross Roads

Some called him the "Wizard of the Saddle," and, by the summer of 1864, many in the North conceded that Nathan Bedford Forrest had earned the name, one that made even his most seasoned opponents nervous. Though he had never studied military science, Forrest had the natural instincts that made him a superior soldier. His strategy and tactics always seemed sound, and he was especially effective in independent command. Whenever he served under someone else, there was usually a blowup. The prime example thus far in the war had been a heated exchange with Braxton Bragg in Georgia. Forrest had raged against Bragg in a personal confrontation and had stormed out of Bragg's tent. Soon afterward, the fiery Forrest had been given an independent command of sorts in Mississippi. (Stephen D. Lee was Forrest's immediate superior, but he wisely left Forrest to carry out orders pretty much in his own way.) The Confederate command structure in the west might be more peaceful with Forrest in Mississippi, but he should have been kept in Georgia where his exploits would have been much more significant.

As it was, William T. Sherman should have been relieved that Forrest was so many miles away. But Sherman was nervous. About to begin his Atlanta campaign, Sherman knew that his long supply line would get ever longer as the Federal army moved into the interior of Georgia. Forrest might be in Mississippi, but he certainly could bring his cavalry to middle Tennessee in a hurry and devastate supply de-

Nathan Bedford Forrest. Confederate cavalryman who won his greatest victory at Brice's Cross Roads. Credit: Ezra J. Warner, *Generals in Gray*, Baton Rouge: LSU Press

pots and rail lines that were essential to the survival of Sherman's force.

On June 1, 1864, Forrest left Tupelo with three thousand cavalry and two artillery batteries, moving toward middle Tennessee just as Sherman had feared. Lee had ordered Forrest to attack "the railroad from Nashville" and to break up "lines of communication connecting that point with Sherman's army in Northern Georgia." Forrest was on his way when he received an urgent message from Lee on the morning of June 3. A large Federal column was on the move from Memphis in the direction of Tupelo; Forrest must return at once.

Led by Samuel Sturgis, the Union column of infantry, cavalry, and artillery, some 8,000 men and 250 wagons, had been ordered into Mississippi for the very purpose of keeping Forrest occupied and destroying him if possible. Sturgis had orders to proceed to Corinth, clear the town of Rebel soldiers, and then move south, tearing up track and burning depots of the Mobile and Ohio Railroad as far

Samuel Sturgis. Defeated by Nathan Bedford Forrest at Brice's Cross Roads. Credit: Ezra J. Warner, *Generals in Blue*, Baton Rouge: LSU Press

south as Macon. Sturgis was given much discretion, and he would use more than he had anticipated.

For one thing the weather, marked by seemingly unrelenting rains, turned roads into quagmires. Sturgis's target was supposed to be Corinth, and to get there he had been instructed to dip down into Mississippi via the now-defunct towns of Salem and Ruckersville in Benton County and then turn northeast to Corinth. He did his best to keep to that route, but the rains slowed the column to a crawl. Union cavalry, led by Benjamin Grierson of Grierson's Raid fame, did reach Corinth, found no Rebels there, and was ordered back to Ripley. From Ripley, the horse soldiers moved south by southeast feeling along the Mobile and Ohio for the enemy.

Meanwhile, the main Federal column paused at Ripley while Sturgis evaluated his options. He called his division commanders together and asked for their opinions. Leading the discussion himself, Sturgis pointed out that the excessive rain—it was still falling—had so slowed the column's progress that the enemy was bound to have a fix on their location. Also, the horses and mules were getting tired, and forage was getting more difficult to find. The consequences of a defeat under such conditions might be devastating. However, others present reminded Sturgis that he had already called off an expedition a few weeks before because of "the destitution of the country." To retreat again without making contact with the Rebels "would be ruinous." Furthermore, all reports indicated that there was no sizable enemy force anywhere in the area. So, Sturgis wrote later, "Under these circumstances, and with a sad foreboding of the consequences, I determined to move forward." Sturgis recognized the necessity of assisting Sherman by drawing Forrest away from the latter's supply line. He also knew that Sherman's wrath could be severe.

On June 7, with great caution and a tight formation, the soaked bluecoats continued on a south/southeasterly course from Ripley, the same route Grierson's cavalry had taken. Sturgis worried because he had received no recent news from Grierson's scouts and had obtained no reliable information from local citizens.

On June 10, the march began early as usual, the cavalry taking the lead at 5:30 a.m. Then came the infantry at 7 a.m.; Sturgis wanted each branch of his force to be clear of the other in case of a Confederate attack. Pioneers assigned to keeping the road clear and checking bridges moved ahead of the infantry. Sturgis rode ahead and found "an unusually bad place in the road, and one that would require considerable time and labor to render practicable." While waiting for the pioneers to get to work, a message arrived from Grierson. The cavalry had encountered enemy cavalry at a place a few miles ahead called Brice's Cross Roads.

On June 7, Bedford Forrest had received scouting reports that the Yankees were in the vicinity of Ruckersville. He had ordered his troops first to Baldwyn, north of Tupelo, and then further north to Booneville. Stephen Lee kept in touch with Forrest and directed all available troops toward the coming showdown. A small Federal detachment had been spotted wrecking track near Rienzi, and Forrest was looking there as he contemplated his next move.

On the evening of June 9, Forrest learned for the first time that Sturgis was veering farther south and had been spotted by Confederate scouts several miles southeast of Ripley on the Guntown road. Forrest reacted at once. Being thoroughly familiar with the area, he knew that if he beat the Yankees to Brice's Cross Roads west of Baldwyn he could block their march. If he fought them there they would also be in a precarious position, because just beyond the crossroads toward Ripley ran Tishomingo Creek. The creek could cause an army retreating from the crossroads severe logistical problems. Orders poured from Forrest's headquarters calling for all his available men to concentrate toward the crossroads. His fighting blood surging, Forrest rode on ahead with his escort on June 10 and learned that the enemy was within four miles of Brice's. He immediately sent one of his staff with a few men from the Seventh Tennessee cavalry ahead to check out the information. He soon received a message that the enemy had been met and shots had been fired.

Forrest had developed a simple but effective plan. The weather was hot and the roads muddy. He would first whip Sturgis's cavalry. Meanwhile, the Union infantry would be rushing forward to the sounds of battle. But the weather and the roads would slow them, and they would arrive in a fatigued condition. This would give the Confederates the advantage, and Sturgis would be totally defeated. It was risky business, for Forrest would be outnumbered in the coming fight by more than two to one. Yet he had supreme confidence in his own ability and the fighting capabilities of his men.

Meanwhile, Sturgis sent word to Grierson not only to hold the crossroads but to drive the enemy back toward Baldwyn. In his postbattle report, Sturgis wrote that he wanted to keep the road to Guntown open so he could reach the railroad. "I did not intend being drawn from my main purpose," said Sturgis.

Fighting dismounted, Forrest's troopers kept on arriving and con-

Brice's Cross Roads Visitor Center, Highway 45 west of Baldwyn. Photo: Michael B. Ballard

tinued to push Grierson's force back toward Brice's. The Confederates threw up breastworks where needed, but in the main kept on the offensive, threatening the Federal flanks and trying to get in the rear of the Union column. The battle heated up toward the early afternoon. At about 1 p.m., Confederate artillery finally arrived, as well as the rest of Forrest's force. The enemy cavalry had already been beaten back and their places in line taken by Sturgis's tired infantry. Forrest knew it was time to make his move.

The wily Tennessean used one of his favorite tactics—the flank attack—to strike the telling blow against Sturgis. Traveling with his escort and one brigade, Forrest rode over to the far left of his line to the Ripley-Guntown road south of Brice's. He left instructions to the commanders in the center and on the right to press the enemy hard once the attack on the left began. Having reached his destination, Forrest at once ordered the assault against Sturgis's right flank. The fight quickly became general and especially vicious on the left.

Sturgis had formed three lines once his infantry had arrived, and the Confederate attack on the Union right began to stall. Forrest

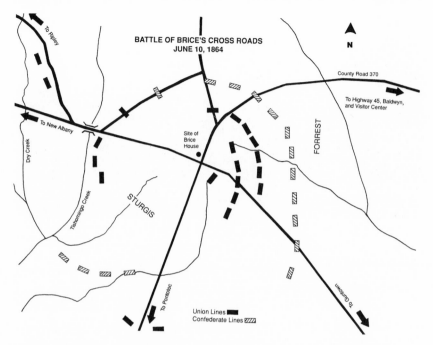

Battle of Brice's Cross Roads, June 10, 1864

then sent orders back to his main line that more pressure had to be put upon the Federal left. Fretting over whether the orders had been received, Forrest rode back over to his right. He personally prepared the attack in that sector, ordering up what few pieces of artillery he had available to break the fierce Yankee resistance. Forrest later wrote, "The battle was fierce and the enemy obstinate; but after two hours' hard fighting the enemy gave way, being forced back on his third and last line."

By this time a Rebel detachment had gotten around the Federal left and was attacking the Union rear, another favorite Forrest tactic, while the rest of Sturgis's line was falling back toward the crossroads. Compounding the slow retreat before Forrest's pressure was the at-

Brice's Cross Roads Battlefield. Photo: Michael B. Ballard

tempt by too many soldiers in blue to get across the Tishomingo Creek bridge just a few yards northwest of the crossroads.

Concerned about his wagon train, Sturgis posted an extra guard of black infantry and portions of Grierson's cavalry to protect the supplies. But his battle lines began to crumble too quickly, and "[o]rder soon gave way to confusion and confusion to panic." Forrest concurred that "the steady advance of my men and the concentrated, well-directed, and rapid fire from my batteries upon that point [the crossroads] threw them back, and the retreat or rout began."

Sturgis noted the time at 5 p.m.; his men, many already exhausted when they reached the battlefield, had nothing left to give. Sturgis mourned that "they were compelled to abandon not only the field, but many of their gallant comrades who had fallen, to the mercy of the enemy. Everywhere the army now drifted toward the rear, and was soon altogether beyond control." With Grierson's help, Sturgis tried to rally his men and was—very briefly—successful. Sturgis recognized that "it was now impossible to exercise any further control. The road became crowded and jammed with troops, the wagons and artillery, sinking into the deep mud, became inextricable, and added to the general confusion that now prevailed. No power could now check or control the panic-stricken mass as it swept toward the rear." He noted disdainfully that one of his colonels rode so hard back toward Ripley that he made ten miles before finally stopping for a rest. Sturgis decided that all he could hope for was to save the troops, so he ordered supply wagons destroyed and artillery disabled. Many wagons and guns, however, because of panic in the Union ranks, were simply abandoned.

Forrest's men had reached their limit, too, but as the Federals fled into the night toward Ripley, he tried to keep up the pressure. The victorious general sent an advance party to scout the enemy's retreat, while his main force rested and ate. Forrest did not wait until daylight of June 11 to renew the pursuit. At 1 a.m. his force was on the road. During these early-morning hours, the Confederates found more abandoned wagons and artillery and twice encountered the enemy drawn up in line of battle. The lines quickly melted away, having obviously been left behind the main column to slow the Rebels.

At 8 a.m. Forrest found the Yankees in considerable force and ready for battle at Ripley. With only a few troops present, he ordered an attack on the Union right flank and set up a skirmish line all along the front. More Confederates arrived, and Sturgis's men began running out of ammunition and gave way. By the time Forrest called off the pursuit, the Federal column was no longer an organized force. Panicky bluecoats fled toward the Memphis and Charleston Railroad and succor behind Union lines. The scattered column arrived at Collierville, Tennessee, on the morning of June 12. A train from Memphis arrived a few hours later, bringing food and reinforcements.

As for Samuel Sturgis, his participation in the war ended when Cump Sherman learned of the debacle at Brice's. Sherman was unimpressed with Sturgis's claim that he had been whipped by fifteen-to-twenty thousand Rebels. Even Sturgis's most modest estimates had Forrest with twelve thousand in the battle, plus two infantry divisions that had been held in reserve. Sturgis surfaced again in 1869 as a colonel in the famed Seventh Cavalry of George Armstrong Custer. Fortunately for Sturgis he was not with Custer at the Little Big Horn.

For Bedford Forrest, the battle at Brice's Cross Roads proved to be the supreme moment of his Civil War career. He had inflicted 2,240 casualties (most of whom were listed as "missing" by Sturgis and "captured" by Forrest) on a superior force while suffering just under 500 himself. His strategy and tactics, studied by military scientists ever since, were practically flawless. In an address to his victorious men, Forrest bragged with good reason that the Federals "became an enemy beaten, defeated, routed, destroyed."

But Sherman had not yet given up his campaign to neutralize, or preferably kill, Forrest. He would soon order another expedition to seek out this Confederate nemesis. This time, in one of the war's many ironies, Forrest would follow his greatest victory with his poorest performance.

EIGHT

Turning the Tables:
The Battle of Tupelo

In the aftermath of the Union defeat at Brice's Cross Roads, Cump Sherman grew more determined than ever to eliminate Bedford Forrest. Sherman was convinced that Forrest was "the very devil" and that there would never be peace in Tennessee until that devil was killed. Forrest had to be erased even if it cost ten thousand lives and wrecked the U.S. Treasury, Sherman wrote to Washington. The fuming Sherman, wishing that he could forget Forrest and concentrate on his Atlanta campaign, set in motion another expedition to do what Samuel Sturgis had failed to accomplish.

As it happened, A. J. Smith, who had served under Sherman during the Meridian campaign, was in Memphis with elements of the XVI and XVII corps. Having just returned from Nathaniel Banks's Red River campaign, another Union debacle, Smith was on his way to the Mobile area to participate in a campaign against that southern port city. Sherman wired Memphis headquarters to forget Mobile. Smith should organize his force at once and go after Forrest.

Smith set to work, and, by early July 1864, was assembling an army at La Grange, Tennessee. On July 5, his army of some fourteen thousand moved toward Mississippi. The column moved very slowly, screened by Benjamin Grierson's cavalry and suffering under the hot Mississippi sun. More than heat slowed the march. Smith was cautious; he did not intend to make Sturgis's mistake of being drawn into battle on the enemy's terms.

Smith's major target, Nathan Bedford Forrest, was aware of an-

Andrew Jackson Smith. Victorious Union commander at the Battle of Tupelo. Credit: Ezra J. Warner, *Generals in Blue,* Baton Rouge: LSU Press

other Yankee invasion, and his scouts kept a close watch on Smith's line of march. The Federal army moved to Ripley, before turning southwest toward New Albany and south to Pontotoc. The enemy's decision to turn surprised Forrest, who had ordered cavalry to Ellistown about halfway between Ripley and Tupelo. This was the straightest route to the railroad and major supply depots, the usual target of Union armies invading northeast Mississippi. Smith had contributed to Confederate confusion by feinting toward Tupelo.

So Forrest had been outmaneuvered, and it would not be the last time during this campaign. Suffering both from painful boils that made riding difficult and from a bruised ego because his immediate superior, Stephen D. Lee, had been appointed lieutenant general first, Forrest had tried to relinquish field command for the next match with the Yankees. But Lee resisted; he knew Forrest's value in the field. Finally a compromise had been reached. Forrest would stay in the field, but Lee would be on hand and in immediate command. Forrest may have figured that since Lee seemed to be getting credit among his West Point cronies in Richmond for the former's victories, he should come to the battlefield and earn his accolades. Whatever the truth was, Forrest's heart was not in this campaign, and his performance would be subpar from the start to the point when he fell wounded.

Smith marched his men on through New Albany, reaching Pontotoc on July 11. There had been skirmishing along the way as Forrest's scouts skirted along the Union flanks, but so far no serious fighting had occurred. At Pontotoc, Smith paused, causing further consternation in Confederate circles. Forrest assumed that Smith must be heading for Okolona, so the Rebels had begun concentrating troops there and digging in to give the invaders a warm reception. Forrest also ordered a roadblock south of Pontotoc on the Okolona road designed both to hold the Federals up while the Confederates got ready at Okolona and to entice Smith to keep moving down the Okolona road.

But Smith did nothing on the eleventh or the twelfth. Forrest began to think that the enemy had gotten cold feet and were going to retreat to Memphis. Meanwhile Lee had arrived at Okolona and had taken command. Forrest briefed him, and they decided to go to the Pontotoc front. An order was canceled to have the troops retreat who had been holding the roadblock south of Pontotoc. When the two generals arrived at the front, they discussed options, finally deciding either to fight Smith at Smith's instigation or attack if the Union column began retreating. In essence, the campaign initiative had been turned over to the Federals.

On the night of July 12, Smith made his decision. Most of his men had had a chance to rest up from the heat, and now it was time to make a move. He would order demonstrations south of Pontotoc the next morning, while his main column turned onto the road east leading to Tupelo. Smith had obviously become convinced that the enemy had been trying to lure him into battle in the direction of Okolona. By marching to Tupelo, he could find a battleground of his own choosing. It would be risky, because he would be vulnerable to flank and rear attacks, but, if he could get a good head start, For-

Stephen D. Lee. Commander of Confederate forces at the Battle of Tupelo. Credit: F. T. Miller, *The Photographic History of the Civil War*, New York: Review of Reviews Co.

rest and Lee would have trouble concentrating forces. Rebel troops were scattered about Pontotoc and would have trouble coordinating their attacks while the Union column was on the move. Also, the bulk of the Confederate force was at Okolona, too far away to thwart or even harass the Federal march.

Early on July 13, the plan went into motion. Before Forrest and Lee quite understood what was happening, Smith's main column was several miles down the road to Tupelo. Lee ordered Forrest to take a detachment and press the Federal rear. Meanwhile, other Confederates would ride northeast and try to hit the Union right flank.

The Union rear was protected by cavalry and several hard-fighting Colored Infantry regiments. Forrest hit them time and again, but soon gained a respect for their soldierly ability. These black regiments developed a tactic of hiding behind advantageous terrain, allowing the pursuing Confederates to get close, and then rising up and opening fire. The Rebels learned quickly and got more and more cautious as the chase to Tupelo continued.

While Forrest punched and counterpunched with the Union rear, other Confederates made an attempt to assault the right flank. At a place called Bartram's Shop (also called Burrow's Shop), a small detachment surprised the Federals and shot several mules, which forced the destruction of a number of supply wagons, a caisson, and a couple of ambulances. The Union troops quickly rallied, flanked the Confederates and forced a retreat after inflicting several casualties. At Coonewah Crossroads, a stronger Rebel force hit the flank, but bluecoats rallied at once to the spot as if drawn by a magnet. These were not the disorganized, panicky troops of Samuel Sturgis. Smith's men were well drilled, cool under fire, and responsive to every emergency.

By day's end, the Confederates had scored a few minor points, but Smith's column had made it. They filed into battle formation behind a high ridge at the once-thriving community of Harrisburg, just west of Tupelo. The railroad had bypassed Harrisburg, and it had died a slow death while Tupelo had grown. But Harrisburg was about to become alive again in a way that the few residents who still lived there did not want. The war was about to come to Harrisburg, and to Tupelo, in a big way.

On the night of July 13, the Confederates gathered in front of the Federals' lines. Lee had about seventy-five hundred men and had to decide what to do next. Clearly, Smith's choice to stop and form a battle line meant that he was inviting an attack. Lee and Forrest had decided to fight Smith if Smith indicated he wanted a fight. That evening the two consulted, and Lee decided to attack the next morning. There is still controversy about whether Forrest agreed with that decision, although Lee claimed in later years that he and Forrest had no disagreement over the plan.

It may be so, but Forrest certainly had his doubts. After his conference with Lee that evening, Forrest suddenly jumped up from his blanket and called to an aide. The two proceeded to ride into the midst of the Union lines and camps. Under cover of darkness, Forrest and his aide traversed enough of Smith's army to get a good idea of his strength. They were once challenged by Federal sentries, but Forrest thundered at them for daring to attempt to stop their commanding officer. By the time the ruse was discovered, the sentries' shots flew wide of the mark as the two Confederates rode hard back to their own lines. Forrest had learned enough to be convinced that the Federals had too many men in too strong a position for a head-on attack. Yet Lee was in charge, and Forrest would follow orders, though his performance the next day indicated that his heart was not in this battle.

The Confederates began forming around 2 a.m., July 14, and at dawn Lee set his attack in motion. Lee would claim in later years that he never had more than sixty-six hundred available for combat, too few to attack an entrenched force of fourteen thousand. Forrest led the initial assault as the Confederate right hammered the Union left. Lee's idea was that Forrest would get around Smith's left all the way to the railroad in Tupelo, thus forcing Smith to abandon his position.

The assault never amounted to much. Forrest did get the orders to the troops on the Confederate right. But while he was making ready the attack in that sector, he noticed that Rebel troops, Kentuckians, near the right center had gotten close to the front and were being rather roughly handled. Forrest rallied them back into formation, but the heat of the Federal fire convinced him he could accomplish nothing. "The terrific fire. . . ," he wrote, "showed that the enemy were supported by overwhelming numbers in an impregnable position, and wishing to save my troops from the unprofitable slaughter I knew would follow any attempt to charge his works, I did not push forward" the attack force on the right when it arrived. There would be a lengthy postwar debate about what Forrest might have done had he fought here as he had fought elsewhere in the war. Smith did not have to worry any further about the classic flank-

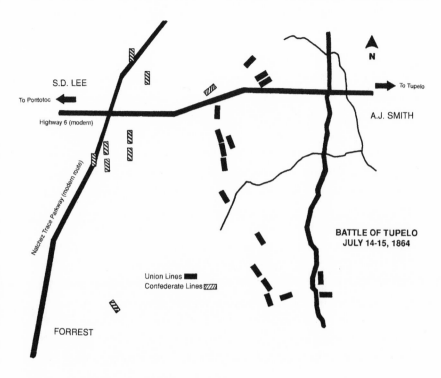

M 8 Battle of Tupelo, July 14-15, 1864

and-rear tactic that Forrest had employed so often. Forrest had made up his mind that it could not be done, and that was that.

Meanwhile, the battle raged along the rest of the line. Confederates charged and invariably were beaten back. Smith described a typical result during a Rebel attack near the Pontotoc road. "They drove in our skirmishers and were allowed to come to within about 100 yards of the main line (which was the First Brigade of the Third Division at this point), when they [Union troops] rose and delivered one volley at short range, and then charged with the bayonet, driving the enemy with heavy loss from the field, killing more even as they were running than they did in the first volley." Again and again, Union troops held their fire until the attacking Confederates were within point-blank range. Then the bluecoats arose and fired, both from the front and often from the flank. The attitude up and down the Union line seemed to be that anyone having a clear shot should fire at the enemy no matter where the attacks were taking place.

It did not take long for the Confederates to realize that Lee had made a mistake ordering an attack here. The Federal lines were too strong and their fire too concentrated for an outnumbered force to break through. Forrest noted hundreds of men simply collapsing from heat exhaustion, as the Rebel lines repeatedly charged and fell back. There were not enough troops to reinforce all the trouble spots. One Confederate commander got three conflicting orders because men were desperately needed all along the line. Finally the Confederates fell back and built breastworks, awaiting the Union countercharges that would surely come.

A. J. Smith was still cautious, however. His men had inflicted heavy casualties on the enemy, and he had seen firsthand how the defending force had the advantage. He had enough respect for the Confederates to keep him from sending his troops out to the attack. He did allow his men to advance and clear the battlefield, picking up wounded Confederates and abandoned weapons. After that, the Union troops retreated to their lines and engaged in skirmishing until dark.

On the Confederate side, Forrest led a reconnaissance in force late in the day against the enemy's left flank. His men drove in the Federal skirmish line but went no farther. According to Forrest, they ran into an "unceasing roar of small-arms" and the "whole line was lighted up by a continuous stream of fire." He said that it was "one of heaviest fires I have heard during the war."

Smith had won the day and probably had visions of a more complete victory on July 15. But a logistical problem changed his mind, and he ordered a retreat. The problem was really inexcusable, but

Smith blamed no one in his battle report. He simply wrote that "much of our bread was spoiled when drawn from the commissary depot, we had on hand but one day's rations left." A further problem was that he had only one hundred rounds of artillery ammunition left. "It, therefore, became," Smith wrote, "a matter of necessity to return." Of course, Smith's army was in a region where they could have lived off the land for several days. Perhaps the supply situation gave him a good excuse to quit while he was ahead.

Leaving his army in battle formation while preparations were made for retreat, Smith ordered Grierson to tear up railroad track on the Mobile and Ohio for five miles north and south of Tupelo. Smith did not mention it, but he had had his men set fire to several houses in the area, too. He was probably merely following Sherman's dictum that southern residents in Forrest territory be reminded that there was a price to pay for supporting "ole Bedford."

In the Confederate lines, Forrest and Lee again waited for Smith to attack, but again in vain. Finally Abraham Buford led an attack on the Federal left, but ran into strong resistance from what amounted to a rear guard. Soon word from Rebel scouts confirmed that the Yankees had departed and were headed northwest up the Ellistown road.

Forrest hastily ordered a pursuit and then met with Lee to discuss the situation. After the conference, Forrest rode toward the sound of firing. He found a hot engagement taking place at Old Town Creek, where the Confederates had caught up with the Union column. Federal commanders sent two brigades and a regiment up the hill where the Rebels were posted. While encouraging his troops, Forrest received a painful foot wound that put him out of action. Their inspirational leader was now gone, and, more important, the Confederates were overwhelmed by superior numbers. They fell back to Tupelo. Elements of Lee's force followed the Federals for two days but could do little damage. Smith and his army arrived back at La Grange on June 21. The Tupelo campaign was over.

During the campaign, Smith had lost just under seven hundred men, while Lee and Forrest had suffered over thirteen hundred casualties. Smith reported three thousand total casualties for Forrest and Lee, but casualty totals given by one side for the other were almost always inflated.

The Federal high command, while disappointed that Forrest had not been destroyed, were pleased with the pounding Smith had administered to the Confederates. Tactically, Lee and Forrest could claim victory since Smith had given up the field, but there had been no doubt among the participants on both sides that the Federals had won at Tupelo (the battle was also known as Harrisburg). And Smith had won in the long view as well, for he had kept Forrest occupied just as Sherman had wanted. Also, he had effectively used the very tactics employed by Forrest in the past: outguessing the enemy, screening his intentions, enticing the enemy into fortified positions, flank firing. In many ways the tables had been turned on Forrest. Furthermore, his wound would keep him out of action for a while.

It turned out to be a very short while, however. Forrest and Smith were both back in the field in August 1864. Sherman, disgusted because Smith had had to retreat from Tupelo, sent word that Smith was to stay after Forrest and keep him busy. Sherman was already on the outskirts of Atlanta, so he was not as apprehensive as he once had been. But he still wanted Forrest occupied. Smith succeeded at that, though his second outing against Forrest was not as successful as the Tupelo campaign had been.

In what might be called a footnote to the Tupelo campaign, Smith led his second expedition against Forrest down into the Oxford area along the Mississippi Central Railroad that ran south from La Grange. (Stephen D. Lee had been ordered to the Georgia front, and Forrest had once more been given free reign in the region.) Forrest realized that he was too outnumbered to give battle, so he decided on one of his trademark daring tactics. Leaving the front, Forrest led a raid on Memphis, causing much consternation there among the occupying Federal force. Smith gave up his raid, after wreaking much destruction, and moved back to La Grange and on to Memphis. Again an effort to get Forrest had failed, but again the overall strategy of keeping Forrest in Mississippi had succeeded.

Skirmishes and movements of troops in Mississippi would continue, but the Tupelo campaign and its aftermath effectively ended major campaigning in the state. Sherman devastated Georgia and then marched up through South Carolina and North Carolina, finally forcing the surrender of the decimated Confederate Army of Tennessee in 1865. Ulysses S. Grant had earlier accepted Robert E. Lee's surrender in Virginia, and for Mississippi and Mississippians the war was finally over. Many long years of rebuilding lay ahead.

SUGGESTIONS FOR FURTHER READING

Bearss, Edwin C. *Forrest at Brice's Cross Roads and in North Mississippi.* Dayton, OH: Morningside, 1979.

Bearss, Margie Riddle. *Sherman's Forgotten Campaign: The Meridian Expedition.* Baltimore: Gateway Press, 1987.

Hattaway, Herman. *General Stephen D. Lee.* Jackson: University Press of Mississippi, 1976.

Hurst, Jack. *Nathan Bedford Forrest: A Biography.* New York: A. A. Knopf, 1993.

Marszalek, John F. *Sherman: A Soldier's Passion for Order.* New York: Free Press, 1993.

Wyeth, John A. *That Devil Forrest: Life of General Nathan Bedford Forrest.* Baton Rouge: Louisiana State University Press, 1989. Reprint.

Conclusion: The Legacy of the War in Mississippi

The Civil War took a heavy toll on Mississippi. Many of the state's political and economic elite either fell in battle or saw their fortunes ruined by the devastation and economic upheaval wrought by the conflict. Some white families managed to hang on to a semblance of their prewar positions; others were ruined. Most members of the white community, in Mississippi and elsewhere in the Confederacy, were simply shocked and overwhelmed by the circumstances of defeat.

Black Mississippians, on the other hand, were overjoyed at being set free by Abraham Lincoln and the Union armies. While still slaves, many set up a sort of underground information network to get the word out about the Emancipation Proclamation. Though freed, some felt loyalty toward their former masters, but for the great majority the end of the war was a time of jubilation. Many felt they had earned their freedom, for, whether acting as spies for Union armies or actually suiting up and serving in black regiments, they had made a direct contribution to Union victory.

Then came Reconstruction, one of the most trying and controversial periods in American history. Early on, the survivors of the white southern power base thought they had a friend in President Andrew Johnson, who seemed to advocate a lenient policy, but he turned out to be unreliable. Then the Radical Republicans took over, and, briefly, carpetbaggers, scalawags, and former slaves played prominent roles in large parts of the South. The perceived detrimental influence of these groups has been overstated and their accomplishments understated. Historians still debate the nuances of the period, but one thing is certain. Southern whites took back power and began a long period of racial recrimination. To them, southern blacks were not just freedmen but were a threat to the old way of life adhered to by whites in Mississippi and other areas of the former Confederacy.

The Mississippi Constitution of 1890 was a landmark event in southern efforts to revoke the citizenship that blacks had gained as a result of the war. Voting laws and other regulations made it nearly impossible for African Americans in the South to maintain their rights as citizens. The 1890 constitution also created a new Mississippi state flag (the current one), which, significantly, has the Confederate battle flag in the upper-left-hand corner.

Mississippi, home of ex-Confederate President Jefferson Davis, was in the forefront of the "Lost Cause" movement that swept the South in the late 1800s. Confederate soldiers and leaders, especially Davis, were memorialized and deified. The Confederate years became exaggerated in the myth of moonlight and magnolias, and whites spoke with reverence of "the war" and all the good things about the South it represented, at least in the minds of Lost Cause adherents. In many states of the old Confederacy, and it seemed especially true in Mississippi, the desire to celebrate the war years led to a yearning for the past and ultimately a firm resolve to cling to an idea of the "good ole days"—no matter what. It became easier to hold on to the notion as time passed, because the North, anxious for reconciliation, abdicated any responsibility for protecting black rights in the South.

As elsewhere in the region, black Mississippians were swept into the background and forced to live a demeaning Jim Crow existence. Mississippi legislatures repeatedly strengthened discriminatory laws over the years, and violence erupted when beleaguered African American citizens challenged the status quo. The underlying thought in the minds of most white Mississippians seemed to be that losing the war did not mean giving up a life divided along racial lines. The "separate but equal" doctrine that was pervasive in the South before the civil rights revolution of the 1960s did little to improve race relations. It quickly became apparent that, in practice, separate but equal meant separate and unequal.

The decade of the 1960s was perhaps more turbulent in Mississippi than in any other southern state. Violence rocked the state, leaving long-lasting scars on its national image. Ku Klux Klan members waving battle flags of the Confederacy wrought such turmoil that it took the power of the federal government, notably the FBI, to bring the situation under control. Toward the end of the decade, court-ordered desegregation of public schools marked a turning point in the state's long wrestling match with the Civil War era.

Since integration, there has been a gradual soothing of the hot passions that so long dominated Mississippi's racial climate. Members of the state's biracial community talk more, interact more, and now and then even vote for one another. The Mississippi state flag, unchanged since 1890, still occasionally causes rancor and debate, as do some of the Confederate memorials that are sprinkled around the state. On the other hand, scattered among the memorials are numerous streets and other areas named in honor of the martyred African American hero Martin Luther King, Jr. There are those who do not feel comfortable with that kind of trade-off, but it indicates progress unthinkable in previous times.

As the twentieth century draws to a close, there is a general sense that most Mississippians would like to let go of the past and move on to solve problems that are more immediate and important than symbols. And there are indications, too, that most Mississippians are ready to put the war in proper perspective. It was a crucial event in American history, and it has much to teach us yet about ourselves as a people. Those who wish to celebrate and honor its memory can do so, however, without hanging onto its coattails.

In recent years the former mayor of Corinth, an African American, joined hands with whites and blacks to work toward a national military park commemorating the Civil War fighting that raged in that city. If the Corinth project is successful, tourist dollars will benefit all the community. That kind of cooperative spirit would probably be celebrated by ancestors of both races. That it is happening in Mississippi indicates that the Civil War heritage is now having a positive effect on the Magnolia State and that Mississippians are pointing to the future rather than clinging to the past.

Touring the War

Iuka is located in the northeast corner of Mississippi at the intersection of highways 72 and 25. The battlefield is southwest of town along Highway 25 and has not been preserved, although a historic marker identifies the general location. Another interesting site near Iuka is the old Eastport area north of town. Civil War ships anchored there, and the surrounding hills are speckled with campsites and fortifications. To retrace the march of the Union army to Iuka from Corinth, follow Highway 72 (Ord's route) and Highway 45 south (Rosecrans's route). To continue following Rosecrans's approach, turn east at Rienzi onto Route 356. Go through Jacinto (or stop and visit the historic courthouse there) to Route 365; turn south and then turn left again onto Route 364. Continue until Highway 25 appears, and turn left (north) into Iuka. For information, contact the Iuka Public Library (662-423-6300).

The historic town of Corinth is situated in northeast Mississippi at the intersection of highways 45 and 72 (east/west). The town still sits at a railroad intersection; the Memphis and Charleston is now called the Southern, and the Mobile and Ohio is the Illinois Central. Several Civil War sites remain, though it has been only in the last couple of decades that the town has made a concerted effort at preservation. A few state historical markers are scattered along streets. At present, a movement is under way to have a national military park designated at Corinth, though this will be difficult since the town's expansion over the years has covered most of the battle sites.

The most impressive site is Battery Robinett, reconstructed on the original ground of the fortification. Standing in Robinett and looking to the northwest, whence the Confederate attack came, a visitor can understand why the attack failed. A beautiful national cemetery containing mostly Civil War dead stands in the south-central part of town. The remains of Civil War entrenchments can be spotted scattered about town; some are marked and some are not.

Places to contact for maps and tourism information include the Northeast Mississippi Regional Library (662-287-7311), the Northeast Mississippi Museum Association (662-287-3120), and the Curlee House (662-287-9501).

THE VICKSBURG CAMPAIGN

Begin at the Vicksburg National Military Park headquarters on Clay Street, about one hundred yards from the appropriate Interstate 20 exit. For information on all aspects of the campaign, and especially to arrange tours, call 601-636-0583. Taking this step will greatly facilitate visits to other areas that were part of the campaign.

Some impressions of the early aspects of the campaign can be gained by driving along Highway 61 north and south along the Mississippi. Cannon along the roadside mark some of the Confederate positions taken to combat the Union navy. Guns up on the bluffs inside park boundaries mark similar sites.

For those interested in the Grant-Sherman campaign of 1862, the place to see in Vicksburg is on Highway 61 north of town where a historic marker gives the general location of Sherman's attack along Chickasaw Bayou. Another event during this period, the sinking of the USS *Cairo,* is dramatized by the salavaged remains of the vessel on display in the park. Adjacent to the ironclad is an excellent museum containing many relics from the *Cairo.* In north Mississippi, Grant's general route south from the Tennessee line is Highway 7 to Grenada. A stop at Holly Springs is recommended. This historic town, the site of Van Dorn's raid, has many antebellum homes and a county museum. For information, contact the Marshall County Museum (662-252-3669).

The only site available for visiting regarding the early 1863 campaign of diversions is Fort Pemberton. Although there are plans to expand this site someday, it is currently very small and features a historic marker. The fort is located in Greenwood, Mississippi, a Delta town at the intersection of highways 82 and 49E. For information, contact Cottonlandia Museum (662-453-0925). Several historic markers are scattered along the routes of Grierson's Raid. The exact route is probably impossible to trace by modern roads. The general trail, beginning at Ripley, is Highway 15 south to Pontotoc, Highway 41 southeast from Pontotoc to Okolona, Highway 45 south from Okolona to its intersection with 82, then west to Starkville. From Starkville, take Highway 25 to Louisville and from there Highway 15 to Newton. From Newton to Hazlehurst, the main trail is now less direct. Today one would have to take Highway 15 south to Bay Springs, then go west on 18 to Raleigh, south on 35 to Mize, and west on 28 to Hazlehurst and on to Union Church. Returning to the railroad at Brookhaven, Grierson went due south along present-day Highway 51 (paralleling I-55) to the Louisiana line. It must be remembered, too, that many of Grierson's troopers frequently deviated from this route along the way.

Information on all phases of Grant's final campaign can be found at the Vicksburg park. A good place to begin a tour is the Grand Gulf State Park (601-437-5911), located a few miles west of Highway 61. Turn off 61 at the park sign just north of Port Gibson. Information on the Port Gibson battlefield can be found at the Grand Gulf park. To get to the battlefield area, turn west off Highway 61 in Port Gibson at the Windsor sign. Follow the paved road on out of town; it follows the route of the old Bruinsburg-Port Gibson road. Markers can be seen along the road, and the ruins of Windsor are adjacent to the road. To get to the battlefield south of this road, a left turn must be made just outside of town. The branch road is difficult to find without previous instructions. Follow this road to the site of Magnolia Church (no longer standing) and to the Shaifer House.

From Port Gibson, take Highway 18 to Raymond. The battle at Raymond occurred on land just south of the town. The site is not well marked, and the battlefield is not preserved. From Raymond, drive into Jackson and visit the Mississippi Department of Archives and History and the Old Capitol Museum located next to each other at the junction of State and Capitol streets (601-359-6850). Here you can find information on Civil War Jackson and Battlefield Park, which commemorates just a small part of the battle of Jackson.

Leave Jackson heading west on Highway 80, which parallels Interstate 20, and go through Bolton and on to Edwards (or take the I-20 exit at Edwards). Champion Hill is located a few miles east of Edwards, while the Big Black battlefield is west of the town. The Raymond road, Route 467, which played a significant role in the Champion Hill battle, runs southeast out of Edwards toward Raymond. The Coker House, an original structure still standing on the battlefield, is on this route just west of Jackson Creek. If you do not have maps from the Vicksburg park, stop and ask directions. The roads around Champion Hill are very confusing.

From Edwards, take either Highway 80 or I-20 into Vicksburg. The park headquarters has a first-class visitor center and maps for touring the park itself, as well as the campaign battlefields of Chickasaw Bayou, Port Gibson, Raymond, and Champion Hill. Before leaving Vicksburg, visit the Old Court House Museum and the many antebellum homes in the area, including Pemberton's headquarters house and the adjacent Balfour House, home of the famous Vicksburg diarist Emma Balfour. Directions to the museum and the homes can be obtained at the park.

THE MERIDIAN, BRICE'S CROSS ROADS, AND TUPELO CAMPAIGNS

The best way to tour the Meridian campaign is to begin on Highway 80 at Vicksburg and follow it all the way to Meridian. This is the basic route Sherman's army took to Meridian, although on their return trip they veered several miles north. Some areas can be reached by turning north off 80. For example, old Hillsboro is north of 80 near Highway 35. Decatur and Union are on Highway 15 north of 80. Reconstructing the return march would require traveling myriad roadways to get to Canton from Meridian. From Canton back to the Vicksburg area, Sherman probably followed the current route of Highway 22 between Canton and Edwards.

Those wishing to trace Sooy Smith's route to his fight with Bedford Forrest at West Point should begin at New Albany; Smith's trail before he reached New Albany has been largely flooded by the Sardis Reservoir. From New Albany, take Highway 15 south to near Houston and turn east on Highway 32, then south on Highway 45 to West Point. The battlefield is about three miles west/southwest of West Point near Highway 50. To view the Yazoo City part of the campaign, go on Highway 3 (turn off Highway 61 just north of Vicksburg), which follows along the Yazoo River, to Yazoo City. Along the way, visitors wanting to glimpse some rugged country traversed by many soldiers should turn right at Satartia and travel to Mechanicsburg to see some of the Mechanicsburg corridor terrain. At Yazoo City there is a historic marker where the Confederate shipyard used to be. Turn onto Highway 16 toward Benton to see some more of the contested ground during the Yazoo campaign. For information on the Yazoo City area, call the Ricks Memorial Library (601-746-5557).

To retrace Sturgis's march to Brice's Cross Roads, start on Highway 4 east of Ripley, then turn right on 370, left on 30, and then right picking up again on Highway 370 to the battlefield. There is an exit to the battlefield off Highway 45 just west of Baldwyn. The current perserved part of the field is a one-acre site at the crossroads under the jurisdiction of the National Park Service. Hundreds of additional acres have been purchased by the Association for the Preservation of Civil War Sites, and it is hoped that eventually a national park can be established. For information, contact the newly established visitor center (662-365-3969).

Smith's route to Tupelo is Highway 370 from Ripley to Highway 30. Turn right and travel to New Albany, then take 15 south to Pontotoc. The road from Pontotoc to Okolona that was partially contested is currently Route 41. The road from Okolona to Tupelo is now Highway 6. There are historic markers in the Pontotoc area. The Tupelo battlefield has long been lost to urban development. The only preserved site is one acre close to downtown Tupelo. This site is governed by the National Park Service. For information, contact the Natchez Trace Visitor Center (662-680-4025).

Major Campaigns and Battles

1862
Corinth Siege: April 29–June 10, 1862
Vicksburg (naval bombardment): May 18–July 26, 1862
Iuka: September 19, 1862
Corinth: October 3–4, 1862
Vicksburg-North Mississippi Campaign: October–December 1862
Holly Springs: December 20, 1862
Chickasaw Bayou: December 27–29, 1862

1863
Vicksburg Campaign (attempts to bypass): January 1–April 30, 1863
Fort Pemberton: March 11–17, 1863
Grierson's Raid: April 17–May 3, 1863
Vicksburg Campaign (Grant's march): May 1–18, 1863
Port Gibson: May 1, 1863
Raymond: May 12, 1863
Jackson: May 14, 1863
Champion Hill: May 16, 1863
Big Black Bridge: May 17, 1863
Vicksburg Siege: May 19–July 4, 1863
Jackson Siege: July 9–16, 1863

1864
Meridian Campaign: February 3–March 5, 1864 (includes battle of West Point)
Brice's Cross Roads: June 10, 1864
Tupelo: July 14–15, 1864

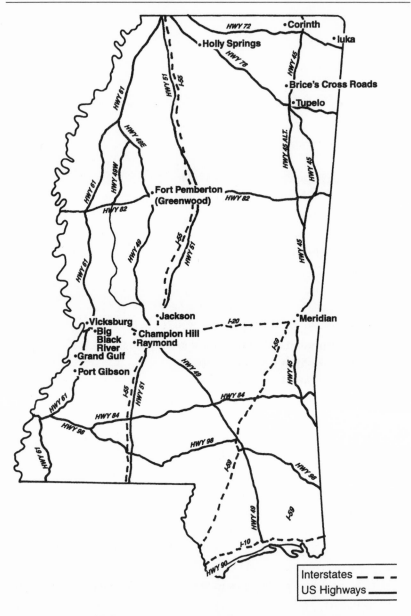

Major Civil War Campaign and Battle Sites in Mississippi

Other Engagements

The following list is selective, not comprehensive, but demonstrates the large number of minor battles and skirmishes that occurred in the state. The cluster of fighting in north Mississippi resulted from Confederate attempts to protect dwindling supply depots vital to Confederate armies in the western theater. Since many sites no longer exist, except perhaps as neighborhoods, the name of the nearest town is given.

1. Abbeville, north of Oxford, August 12, 23, 1864
2. Ashwood, south of Woodville, June 25, 1864
3. Austin, southwest of Tunica, August 2, 1862
4. Baldwyn, June 9, October 2, 1862
5. Barton Station, north of Byhalia, April 16, October 20, 1863
6. Bay Springs, east of Booneville (consumed by the Tennessee-Tombigbee Waterway), October 26, 1863
7. Benton, May 7, 1864
8. Birmingham, west of Saltillo, April 24, 1863
9. Blackland, west of Booneville, June 4, 1862
10. Bolton, July 4–5, 16, 1863, February 4, 1864
11. Booneville, May 30, July 1, 1862, May 7, 1864
12. Brandon, July 18–20, 1864
13. Brownsville, June 18, October 16–18, 1863, September 28, 1864
14. Byhalia, October 12, 1863
15. Canton, July 17–18, September 28, 1863, February 27–28, 1864
16. Canton (15), Brownsville (13), and Clinton, October 15–18, 1863
17. Cherry Creek, north of Pontotoc, July 10, 1864

18. Chulahoma, southwest of Holly Springs, November 30, 1862
19. Chunky Station (Chunky), between Newton and Meridian near I-20, February 12, 1864
20. Clinton, July 8, 16, October 17, 1863, February 5, July 4, 7, 1864
21. Coldwater, May 11, July 24, September 10, November 8–9, 29, 1862, February 19, April 19, July 28, August 21, 1863
22. Coleman's Plantation, near Port Gibson, July 4–5, 1864
23. College Hill, northwest of Oxford, August 21–22, 1864
24. Collinsville, north of Meridian, June 23, 1864
25. Como, October 7, 1863
26. Danville, south of Corinth, June 6, 1864
27. Decatur, February 12, 1864
28. East Pascagoula, near Pascagoula, April 9, 1863
29. Eastport, northeast of Iuka, October 10, 1864
30. Egypt Station (Egypt), December 28, 1864
31. Ellistown, northwest of Tupelo, June 16, 21, 1864
32. Farmington, east of Corinth, May 3, 9, 26, 28, 1862
33. Fayette, November 22, December 22, 1863, October 3, 1864
34. Franklin, northwest of Pickens, January 2, 1865
35. Glendale (Glen), southeast of Corinth, May 8, 1862
36. Greenville, May 20–27, 1864
37. Grenada, August 13, 1863
38. Guntown, May 4, 1863, June 10, 1864
39. Hernando, April 18, May 28, June 20, 1863
40. Hudsonville, northeast of Holly Springs, November 8, 1862
41. Hurricane Creek, northeast of Quitman, August 14, 16, 22, October 23, 1864
42. Ingram's Mill, southeast of Hernando, October 12, 1863
43. Jacinto, August 13, 1863
44. Jumpertown, northwest of Booneville, November 5, 1862
45. Lauderdale, northeast of Meridian, February 15, 1864
46. Liverpool Heights, south of Yazoo City, February 3, 1864
47. Livingston, south of Canton, March 27, 1864

48. Marietta, east of Baldwyn, August 31, 1862
49. Marion, northeast of Meridian, February 17, 1864
50. Mississippi City, between Gulfport and Biloxi, March 8, 1862
51. Morton, February 7–8, 1864
52. Natchez, November 11, December 7, 10, 1863
53. New Albany, April 19, October 5, 1863, July 10, 1864
54. Newton Station (Newton), April 24, 1863
55. Oakland, northeast of Coffeeville, December 3, 8, 1862
56. Okolona, Ivey's Hill, Prairie Mount (latter two northwest of Okolona), February 22, 1864
57. Oxford, December 3, 1862, August 12, 19, 22, 23, 1864
58. Palo Alto, northwest of West Point, April 21–22, 1863
59. Pass Christian, April 4, 1862
60. Plentitude, southeast of New Albany, July 10, 1864
61. Pontotoc, July 11, 1864
62. Prairie Station, north of West Point, February 20, 1864
63. Queen's Hill, northwest of Bolton, February 4, 1864
64. Richmond, south of Mooreville, June 14, 1863
65. Rienzi, August 19, September 9, 18, 1862
66. Rienzi and Kossuth, August 26, 1862
67. Ripley, July 7, December 1, 1863, June 7, 11, July 7, 1864
68. Rodney, southwest of Port Gibson, March 4, 1864
69. Rolling Fork, November 22, 1864
70. Senatobia, May 25, 1863
71. Sharon, northeast of Canton, February 27, 1864
72. Vaughn, east of Benton, May 12, 1864
73. Wall's Bridge, near Magnolia, May 1, 1863
74. Waterford (Lumpkin's Mills), south of Holly Springs, November 29–30, 1862
75. Water Valley, December 4, 1862
76. Woodville, October 6, 1864
77. Wyatt, Lafayette County (consumed by Sardis Reservoir), February 5, 1864

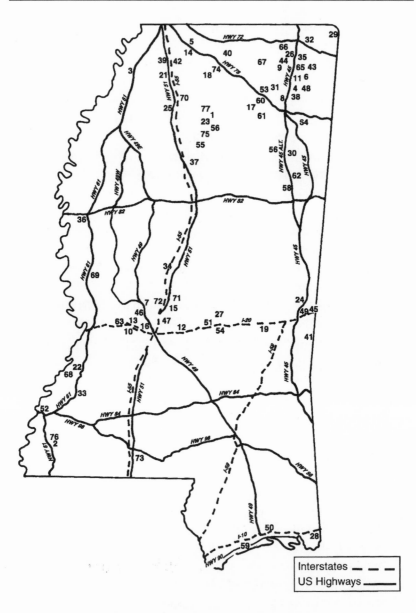

Other Engagements in Mississippi

Civil War Cemeteries

There are very few Mississippi cemeteries of nineteenth-century origin that do not contain the remains of at least one Confederate soldier. Many graves are not in cemeteries. For example, several unknown soldier Union marked graves can be found on an old roadbed adjacent to Highway 41 between Okolona and the Natchez Trace. These men were victims of action against the cavalry of Nathan Bedford Forrest. Many such graves, Confederate and Union, marked and unmarked, are scattered across the state. The list below, compiled by Richard Cawthon of the Mississippi Department of Archives and History, is not intended to be comprehensive; it focuses on the most significant Civil War cemeteries in Mississippi.

CONFEDERATE

Aberdeen: Confederate section of Old Aberdeen Cemetery

Archusa Springs near Quitman: Confederate cemetery

Baldwyn, Brice's Cross Roads Battlefield: Confederate graves in Bethany Cemetery

Biloxi: Confederate cemetery at Beauvoir, last home of Confederate President Jefferson Davis

Brookhaven: Confederate section of Rose Hill Cemetery

Canton: Confederate section of city cemetery

Castalian Springs near Durant: Confederate section of Wesley Chapel Cemetery

Clinton: Unmarked Confederate burial sites in city cemetery

Coffeeville: Confederate graves in city cemetery

Columbus: Confederate section of Friendship Cemetery

Corinth: Graves at Fort Robinett

Crystal Springs: Confederate section of city cemetery

Duck Hill: Confederate cemetery

Enterprise: Confederate section of city cemetery

Grenada: Confederate section of Odd Fellows Cemetery

Hazlehurst: Confederate section of city cemetery; several Union soldier graves nearby

Hernando: Confederate section of Hernando Memorial Cemetery

Iuka: Confederate mass grave at Shady Grove Cemetery

Jackson: Confederate section of Greenwood Cemetery

Lauderdale Springs near Lauderdale: Confederate cemetery

Macon: Confederate section in Odd Fellows Cemetery

Magnolia: Confederate section of city cemetery

Newton: Confederate cemetery

Okolona: Confederate cemetery

Oxford, University of Mississippi campus: Confederate cemetery

Pontotoc: Confederate section of city cemetery

Raymond: Confederate section of city cemetery, enclosed by iron fence

Vicksburg: Confederate section, known as "Soldiers' Rest," of city cemetery

West: Confederate graves at Wheeling Cemetery near West

Winona: Confederate section of Oakwood Cemetery

UNION/NATIONAL CEMETERIES

Corinth: Corinth National Cemetery

Hazlehurst: City cemetery in section adjacent to Confederate section

Macon: Odd Fellows Cemetery in section adjacent to Confederate section

Natchez: Natchez National Cemetery

Vicksburg: Vicksburg National Cemetery located in Vicksburg National Military Park

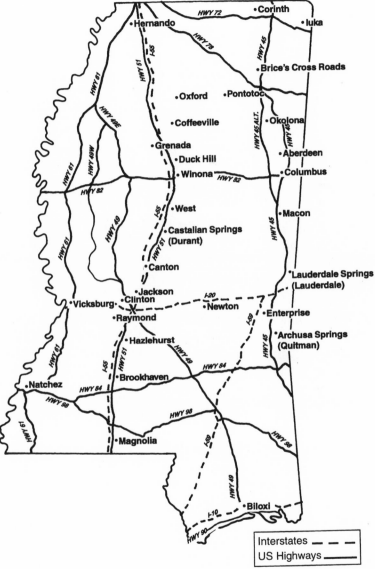

Location of Significant Civil War Cemeteries in Mississippi

Other Places to Visit

ABERDEEN
Many antebellum homes. For information, call the Evans Memorial Library at 662-369-4601.

BEAUVOIR
Last home of Confederate President Jefferson Davis, located on the beachfront in Biloxi. For information, call 1-800-570-3818 or 228-388-9074.

COLUMBUS
Many antebellum homes, including the postwar home of Confederate Lieutenant General Stephen D. Lee. For general information, call 1-800-327-2686 or 662-329-1191. The Lee home phone number is 662-327-8888.

FORT MASSACHUSETTS
Located on Ship Island in the Gulf of Mexico some twelve miles south of Biloxi. Initially occupied and then abandoned by Confederate forces, the fort and island were used as a staging area for the successful attack on New Orleans in 1862. Afterward the site became a prisoner-of-war facility. For tour information, call 1-800-388-3290.

NATCHEZ
Location of some of the most spectacular antebellum homes in the South. For information, call 1-800-647-6724 or 601-446-6345.

ROSEMONT

Boyhood home of Jefferson Davis, near Woodville. For details, call the Woodville Public Library, 601-888-6712.

Index